Want to compete? This is  petitor, starting out this be Coaches are essential and help tremendously! Sometimes they can accidentally overlook something critical in the process assuming the competitor should know or already does. That is why this book was made! With the amount to things to think about and remember, it is next to impossible to absorb it all. I highly encourage anyone thinking about doing a show whether a new or seasoned competitor to buy this book. It is guaranteed you will get outstanding value from the book no matter what your experience level is. Job well done with no detail left out.

—Matt Storm, GBO Pro Men's Beach Body Athlete
GBO Certified Judge
GBO Arizona/California State Director

Storm Classic/Global Open/Global Invitational Promoter
If competing in bodybuilding is on your bucket list, you need to read this book first. Providing perspective from "behind the glitter & tan" as a novice competitor herself, Rian captures the journey of competition prep from beginning to completion with clarity, humor, and honest advice. In my role as a competition coach, I frequently encounter athletes who are ill-prepared for navigating the complexities of competition prep, leading to a negative overall experience. Competing should be an amazing experience of growth and self-confidence! Candid, thoughtful and heartfelt, this book provides helpful guidance, tips, and encouragement to readers who are considering taking the stage.

-Melanie Daly ~ PNBA Pro Figure, NFF & GBO Pro Women's Physique, Founder/Lead Coach of Bodyworx Fit: Be Well * Be Fit * Be Fierce

I can attest from hours of research as well as my own experience in competing that this statement is absolutely true. Every competitor on stage will have a nice set of abs, a great chest, and nice quads, but the competitors who bring a well-developed back side are the ones who separate themselves from the rest and typically bring home the win!

—Mike Lipsey, GBO Pro Men's Beach Body Athlete, Owner Iron Freak Fitness

Sixteen Weeks

The Physique Athlete's Guide
to a **Perfect Prep**

Rian Andrea
NASM-CPT, Pn1

Publication date: December 2020
ISBN Print: 978-1-7359532-0-5
ISBN eBook: 978-1-7359532-1-2

Library of Congress Control Number: 2020922774

This Book is for Educational Purposes Only

This publication is designed to provide accurate and authoritative information in regard to the subject matter covered within the book. This book does not replace the advice of any professional It is sold with the understanding that the author or the publisher is not engaged in rendering any type of legal, medical, or professional information. If expert assistance is required, the services of a competent competition Prep Coach should be sought.

1. Bodybuilding 2. Bodybuilding Prep 3. Sixteen Weeks 4. Physique 5. Bodybuilding Show Prep 6. Women's Bodybuilding 7. Women's Figure 8. Women's Bikini

I Andrea, Rian L. II Sixteen Weeks: The Physique Athletes Guide to a Perfect Prep

Sixteen Weeks: The Physique Athletes Guide to a Perfect Prep may be purchased at special quantity discounts for Competition Prep Coaches, bodybuilders, gyms, training facilities, bodybuilding organizations, and industry related businesses as well as U.S. trade bookstores and wholesalers. Contact Rian at rian@thephysiqueathlete.com

Cover, Layout and Design: Megan Leid
Editors: Mel Cohen, Megan Leid
Publishing Consultant: Mel Cohen of Inspired Authors Press LLC
    inspiredauthorspress.com
Contact Rian for Rights or Licensing Agreements:
    rian@thephysiqueathlete.com
Publisher: The Physique Athlete, LLC
Website: www.thephysiqueathlete.com
Printed in the United States of America

Acknowledgments

I want to thank Scott and Lisa Ramsey of Ramsey Events LLC, Show Glow Competition Services, Bella Glam Mobile Beauty, LLC, and Liquid Sunrays Texas for the invitation to work the Dallas Europa with them. On the day I showed up in Dallas at the Kay Bailey Hutchinson Convention Center, I had no idea that some of the best chapters in this book would be written from what I learned during those two days.

Had I not been there, this book would have never been written. I thought I had experienced a hard day's work before, but tanning, gluing, and glazing over 250 bodies gives a hard day's work a whole new meaning. Y'alls work ethic is insane!

If you ever have the opportunity to experience the joy, love, beauty, grace, and professionalism that exude from these two wonderful people, take it, or you will be missing out. Treat yourself to their services.

A special thanks to my aunt, Regina, for her resolute support of whichever direction I ever wanted to go in life. I could call her right now and tell her I just landed on the moon and I'm thinking of starting an herb garden, and not once would she question how I got there, or why I was on the moon in the first place; she'd only ask why I didn't tell her first and then she'd support the plan by ensuring that the appropriate research and development was being done. That makes me smile and laugh out loud at the same time. Support like that doesn't come around very often.

A very special thank you to Jolinda Hogan for beating my face to death! The baseball cap came off that day. Only for you. I have never looked that good.

To my best friend Dani, for telling me, "You're only thinking locally, you need to create a brand that could be national or international one day." Since we were six months old, she's always been the boss of me. Thank you for being the boss of me that day.

To Annette Richardson – when I was twenty two years old she said, "Pick up the weights and give me some walking lunges, down and back. Go ahead. Do it." I just stood there and looked at her, but I could tell in her expression, I wasn't getting out of it. Thank you for not letting me off the hook.

Thank you the GBO for creating an Athletes First! environment, and the NFF, INBA PNBA, OCB and NPC for creating a space for athletes to work on becoming the best versions of themselves.

I am eternally grateful for my coach, Melanie Daly, for running an unforgivingly tight ship. Not everybody can handle that, but that's exactly what I needed. I desperately needed someone to put boundaries around my entire life, and someone to tell me "No." She said I was going to compete and I had no choice! She met with me every Wednesday morning at 6:00 am for two years, just to get the foundation of my body prepared to go through a prep.

I'm forever indebted to Team Bodyworx Fit; thank you for allowing me to travel with you.

Thanks to Amy Stevens at Gallaudet University who, upon graduation, handed me a $300 check and said, "Go take a writing class."

Thank you to Mel Cohen and Megan Leid for the many many hours of editing, proofreading and layout to deliver you, the reader, a perfect experience.

Dedication

This book is dedicated to Dr. Donna Ryan at Gallaudet University for telling me I needed to find a quiet place to sit and write. I found a quiet place, I wrote, and through your encouragement, I authored this book.

Contents

Preface

I am writing this book after experiencing one full bodybuilding season. The bodybuilding season usually runs from March through November, with the possibility of one or two additional shows in early December.

In the middle of my first competitive bodybuilding season, my mother passed away. A few months later, four weeks out from my stage debut at Lone Star Muscle Mayhem, I was rear-ended in a car accident which resulted in a severe concussion that required four weeks of healing. Still, I completed my personal training certification from the National Academy of Sports Medicine, my nutrition certification from Precision Nutrition, completed my first sixteen-week prep, and competed in my first bodybuilding show where I won first place in Open, Novice, and Master.

In the midst of it all, I travelled as a silent observer with Team Bodyworx Fit, a mighty team out of Georgetown, Texas led by Melanie Daly. I was given the opportunity to learn tanning, glazing, and gluing with Scott and Lisa Ramsey of Liquid Sun Rays Texas and Bella Glam Competition Services, both industry specialists in competition prep.

This book is written for the hundreds of thousands of athletes who dedicate themselves daily to the lifestyle and craft of bodybuilding, and the countless individuals who want to compete one day. This book is for fathers who have raised their daughters to be mentally tough, and for the mothers who don't understand why you would want to look like that, for the brothers and sisters who wish they could one day, and for the proud sons and daughters who cheer for us in the audience. For the people who say, "I just want to do it once."

Readers should select this book for themselves at the first thought of competition, or for a family member thinking about taking up bodybuilding as a sport. If the thought has entered your mind, bodybuilding is in your future. If you are a coach or fitness professional, use this book as a tool for the novice members of your team. This book is for them. If you have a friend that has mentioned bodybuilding, fitness, or follows fitness influencers on Instagram, read this book; you are in the right place!

This book provides valuable insight to entering the world of bodybuilding. There are so many aspects of the industry to discover. As these topics arise, this book gives you a template to read from. *Sixteen Weeks* is meant to be used as a reference guide, and is small enough to throw in your gym bag, yet comprehensive enough to provide valuable insight into the world of bodybuilding for a beginner.

Foreword

By Scott & Lisa Bella Ramsey
Owners of Bella Glam and Show Glow Competition Services

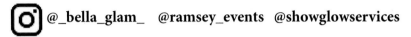 @_bella_glam_ @ramsey_events @showglowservices

From the very first time we met Rian; we knew she was a hard-working, driven person. Knowing she was a competitor herself, we immediately acknowledged that she had a drive many people do not. A drive which requires extreme attention to detail, time management, and insane amounts of sacrifice.

We saw those character traits within her immediately, and knew she would make it extremely far in this industry, which is often oversaturated with athletes. These factors, coupled with the fact that she has a warm, genuine heart that enjoys giving back in a selfless manner, would undoubtedly lead to her be an absolute success in the fitness industry.

Rian took on the task of learning about the industry by engaging with experts, and immersing herself in the field. For starters, she obtained one of the top trainers in the industry. Rian then initiated engagements with experts in the industry either via social media or in person at a show or expo. She learned to identify who was successful in the industry and mirroring them by volunteering to work with these experts. Rian did this in an effort to learn from the best, and also to understand the mindset of what it takes for a successful person or business to excel above the rest.

Chapter 1

BODYBUILDING PICKED ME

The ascetic lifestyle has always fascinated me. Buddhist monks and other spiritual people who chose, for whatever reason, not to drink alcohol, smoke, or watch television. Vegetarians and the real vegans are other examples. Those people who really and truly have "given up" something for what they feel will allow them to gain something better, or to stay on a straight and narrow path. Those who chose not to drink and smoke fascinate me because, as Americans, drinking and driving is almost like a rite of passage. Smoking your first cigarette in high school is what all the cool kids are doing. So many Americans get off work and either stop for Happy Hour on the way home to watch the nightly news, spend a tiny bit of time with the family and then go to bed. And tomorrow, they do the same thing all over again.

The ascetic lifestyle suggests the practice of severe self –discipline and abstention from all forms of self–indulgence. I have always wondered how, in a world where everybody's doing it (which seems to be the motto for human behavior), people still chose ascetic lifestyles. Maybe the most mysterious, and often taboo, lifestyle is the bodybuilding lifestyle. This lifestyle, at its core, is ascetic.

The ascetic lifestyle suggests the practice of severe self-discipline and abstention from all forms of self-indulgence.

A practice that requires an incredible amount of discipline, almost zero self-indulgence or self-indulgent behavior, and full focus on your agreed upon discipline. Bodybuilding is no different. The core of bodybuilding is a type of ascetic lifestyle.

I chose this sport, or shall I say this sport chose me, purely and simply because every day when my feet hit the ground, I know exactly what it is I'm supposed to do. I know which body part is going to be exercised, and I know what I am supposed to eat. From there, I proceed with the day's activities. Not until the act of exercising specific body parts under heavy weight has been completed have I fulfilled the minimum requirements of the day.

Therein lies confidence.

When I first embarked on this journey, I knew I wanted to be and would be successful. I knew I would be good at it. Not only do I have the physical structure and dimensions for bodybuilding, I have the mindset for it.

Chapter 2

WHAT PEOPLE DON'T SEE:
THE PRICE, THE COST, THE VALUE

There's a lot of noise out there. And everybody is an expert.

The internet doesn't need another twenty-something fitness model in fancy leggings and an oversized booty standing in front of a mirror in a sexy pose making duck lips, taking a selfie, and telling you, "You too can look like this if you just train your glutes." People don't deserve that. People deserve to know the actual price, cost, and value of shifting your entire life to achieve a lifelong dream. People deserve to know about the mental preparation required prior to stepping on the competition stage. And not just the competition stage, but the price in dollars, the cost in time and energy, and the value of anything in this life that you want to achieve.

Bodybuilding is an expensive sport, and an expensive sport with little to no tangible return on investment other than a medal or a trophy, and that's a maybe. The real return on investment is the empowering transformation of your mind.

From November 8, 2017 to July 27, 2019, a total of 20 months, I kept a tally of the price, cost and value of bodybuilding to me.

The Price

Weekly personal training sessions	$7,077
Groceries	$5,250
Meals prepped and consumed	2,520
Gym Membership	$944
Supplements	$1,260
Hours of training myself in the gym	858
Eggs consumed	1,512

Eggs receive a special delineation because I don't like eggs, but to achieve my goal, I ate them anyway.

Competition cost	$1,157

> Bodybuilding is an expensive sport, and an expensive sport with little to no tangible return on investment, other than a medal or a trophy, and that's a maybe. The real return on investment is the empowering transformation of your mind.

The Cost

- Two happy hour "friends" who disappeared because I decided drinking wasn't good for me anymore. My goals became my priority.

- My mother passed away from a rare stomach cancer. I was on stage a year to the day of her funeral.

- Two major injuries kept me out of the gym a combined six weeks during prep. Any competitor knows those six weeks are prime training time.

- One concussion four weeks out from my first competition.

- The day I walked into the gym and said "Coach, I ate six slices of pizza for dinner." I had a moment. I was over prep. Over it. My old self showed up.

- The night I sat in the H-E-B parking lot and ate an entire rotisserie chicken.

- At least seven major meltdowns that included some serious tears which most often involved my mind telling me, "You're not good enough, this is too much, why are we doing this anyway?"

The Value

- I got to see my own life come full circle. I watched myself set a goal, make the necessary adjustments to my entire life to start to make room for that goal, get the education I needed to begin the process, and see it through to the very end with medals in my hand.

- I learned how valuable and powerful a tool the mind truly is. Whatever it is you say you can do—no matter what happens, through all of life's challenges—it can be done. Your mind is your only barrier.

Chapter 3

MY BODY, MY BUSINESS, MY BANK ACCOUNT

People see you where you are now, and begin following you on your journey from where you are now. Let me explain. When my clients would come to me, they assumed I had always looked like this. I would often hear, "Well this isn't hard for you. You've always been an athlete." It was shocking to me to hear that in a world of almost eight billion individuals, people would sit across from a desk and tell me that I, and only I, was given a special gift to adhere to a fitness regimen, day in and day out, without fail.

I'm sure you can relate to the things people say that greatly diminish the amount of work it really takes to get the look, and then keep the look.

I call those statements diminishing, because people see a strong, sturdy physical structure and often, if not always, assume there is a stroke of luck given to the individual. I don't possess any extra special powers or specific gifts. It's discipline! Discipline is a learned behavior. It is not where I or anyone else that has the look started. The journey did not start the day you met them. It takes years of dedication to build, then carve, then craft a physique. For me, this season of my life has been over seven years in the making.

I started off as a school teacher. I wanted something and I knew in order to obtain it, I'd have to give something up in exchange for my comfort. To be successful in this business, I knew I needed a strong foundation, a mentor, and a coach. What I needed came in the form of physical training, and I knew I would have to pay for it. For me, the exchange was the comfort of a nicer living space.

I lived in a 250 square foot room with one bed, one sink, a refrigerator and a microwave. The sink was in the bathroom. I lived like that for eighteen months simply because the rent was $550 a month. I was too embarrassed to have friends over. I didn't have many anyway so it didn't matter much. My 250 square foot living space was basically a shed turned living space. And it wasn't one of those fancy schmancy places you'd see on HGTV. The ones where you would say, "Awww that's so cute." Nah, it wasn't that. It was a shed in someone's back yard. It was literally a shed with a bed and a long sofa table.

My training, food, and supplements alone totaled close to $1,000 a month, almost twice my rent. The switch had flipped, I did not care about anything, and I mean anything, other than my training, my fitness goals, and learning the business. Everything I "cooked" was microwaved. Only having access to a microwave meant my diet was frozen veggies, frozen rice, anything steamable, or a whole rotisserie chicken. That was my diet and the microwave was my only tool, but there on that long sofa table, I perfected the art of meal prep. At that time, all I allowed myself access to was physical training and books. At one point, I lived an hour from the gym. According to my calculations, the money spent on gas was cheaper than finding an apartment closer to the gym.

I would go to the gym and lift in the same sweatpants and same sweatshirt day in and day out. I had to learn the discipline of training six days a week. If I had to train in the morning, I would sleep in my training clothes the night before. I used every trick in the book to simplify my process and minimize my own made up excuses. There was nothing pretty about this. Everything smelled. There was nothing cute, and absolutely nothing worth posting on Instagram. There was nothing glamorous about eating six meals a day. The sixth meal was generally the soggiest and most disgusting because it had been in the Tupperware® container the longest. The same chicken, the same broccoli, the same rice, the same food day in and day out. There was nothing about those days of consecutive action that warranted likes or favorites, shares or follows. Nothing. Nobody cared that I was working on my glutes, and they certainly weren't being mentioned in a Drake song. Nobody cared about my beautiful meal prep containers laid out on the counter. I never took a single picture. It was the same six meals, in the same order, in the same leaky Tupperware® for eighteen months. The daily grind wasn't pretty.

I remember being ruthless about eating my food. I set timers on my phone to sound off every three hours. So often I hear from clients, "I can't find time to eat during my day." "I have meetings and I don't want to be eating in front of people."

A: Find time.

B: That's on you.

Sit in the back and eat your food. I distinctly remember going into the bathroom stall at work and eating – yes, at that moment, the only way I could get away was to literally go to the restroom. No one would bother me there. Disciplined! Ruthless! Aggressive! These aren't words typically used in the female vocabulary, but these are the only words your goals will understand.

Some years back, I listened to an interview with IFBB professional bodybuilder Kai Greene, and he said, "Your goal should be so big, when you tell people, they laugh at you." A co-worker caught me leaving the bathroom and asked,

"Did you just eat in there?"

I said, "Yup!" and kept walking.

She laughed. "Perfect," I thought, "I'm on the right track." I had a phenomenal coach, who from the very beginning drilled a hole in my head about my nutrition. "You can be in the gym all day long, but if you don't check your nutrition it won't matter."

My translation, "You're in the gym with a trainer for one hour, you're with yourself the other 23. So, when you get frustrated and all turned inside out, it's you."

Just like the three branches of government, I established for myself a series of checks and balances to help me continue moving in the right direction: my body, my business, and my bank account. In short, these three aspects of my life had to be congruent with one another to see myself through and to this goal.

I urge you to take a real inventory of what you're willing to give up and sacrifice for longer than 21 days. I urge you to figure it out and get to work!

Chapter 4

IT'S EXPENSIVE!

Bodybuilding is an expensive sport. It's an expensive sport with little to no tangible return on investment, other than a medal or a trophy, and that's a maybe. We pay a high price simply out of love. I was so focused on doing the grunt work in the gym, I almost forgot to shift into what I call icing on the cake mode. That is where the bulk of your money is going to be spent.

Let's get down to it. My first piece of advice here is to start saving your money now. Start by putting away about one hundred dollars a month. Approximately half of your expenses will occur during your 16-week prep and the other half are show day expenses, which will occur in the last 72 hours leading up to the stage.

Prep Expenses

1. Shoes $100 —You will basically be shopping for stripper shoes. I've intentionally listed shoes at the top of the list, because aside from being in the gym, your shoes are the next piece of equipment you will be spending the most time in—more than even your suit.

2. Accessories $250—I am not much for coordinating any-thing but jeans and a t-shirt, so I used a company called Competition Kit that allowed me to purchase everything at once—earrings, rings, bracelets, and slippers. Find a company like this, it's worth it.

3. Suit $350–$500—I am intentionally listing your compe-tition suit in your first round of expenses for two main reasons – you will need to get on your designers' calen-dar, and you will need to send her a deposit.

4. Division Fees $100—For each category you enter, you will pay a division fee. In my division, I entered three categories: Novice, Open, and Master. Therefore, I paid $100 for each division, totaling $300.

5. Organization Card $100—This expense snuck up on me because I didn't know about it. Actually, in some cas-es, before you are even able to register for your division and pay for your categories, you will need to purchase your organization card. Each organization has different set fees, but $100 is a reasonable expectation. Unless the organization outlines something different, expect to receive your card in the mail. It's actually pretty exciting to receive and carry it in your wallet!

6. Competition Shorts $100—For my guys, make sure you know which style trunks your division requires. I highly recommend shopping with Chula Wear!

7. Haircut $50—If you do not have a regular barber, get one and get a good one; now is the time to get a good fade. Don't play around with this. I am intentionally listing

these expenses early on, because you and your barber need time to get on the same page. Do several trial runs!

8. Additional Supplements $100—This line item depends a lot on your coach. But just so you have some advanced warning, you may have a few additional supplements to purchase, such as your herbal diuretics and digestive enzymes. These are supplements that you will not need and should not be using until instructed by your coach.

9. Hotel Accommodations $300—If you are able, stay at the host hotel for two nights: the night before the show and the night of the show. You will be exhausted, and being able to stay put after your victory dinner is nice.

Show Day Expenses

These expenses are what I like to call the icing on the cake. This is the moment you have been waiting for!

1. Polygraph $100—Some, not all organizations will require a polygraph. This mostly applies to organizations that have a Natural division under their umbrella.

2. Wax $150—Be sure to wax low enough and high enough.

3. Nails $150—The last time I had my nails professionally manicured, I was eighteen. So of course, twenty years later, I had to do it big! I wanted diamond studs on each nail. I had no idea how much that was going to cost me. I was prepared to pay the 1999/early 2000s price. Little did I know! Think about how your nails are going to match your suit and set money aside accordingly.

4. Hair & Makeup $250–$350—Often you are able to purchase hair and makeup as a package deal. During the off season, I'm a jeans, T-shirt, and a baseball cap girl. So, for me to be able to sit in one seat and pay one person to do both my hair and makeup was magical.

5. Tan $150 cash—Typically, tanning occurs the evening before, around the same time as Athlete Check-In. You will be given an appointment time. Be prepared to hand the tanning company cash money before you step into the spray tent.

6. Peak Week Food $100—In the last two weeks leading up to your show, your coach may begin to reintroduce some foods into your diet that you were restricted during the earlier stages of prep. Be prepared to add those items to your grocery list again.

7. Tickets for your fans $100–$200—Unfortunately, I've heard lots of criticism about the price of entry for bodybuilding shows. Again, defer to the title of this chapter. It's expensive all around. This is a sport where you literally have to pay to play.

I almost forgot! Plan for a small post-show celebration: a little food and couple of drinks. Your fan club should definitely sponsor this event!

Chapter 5

DON'T WORRY, YOU WON'T

At least once a week, I would sit across the desk from a client in a consult, almost always female. For one reason or another, she would express her desire to begin a strength training program. Either doctor recommendation, a friend does it, she has dreams of becoming the next InstaFit influencer, or because Kim Kardashian says so. Either way, most often I hear, "But I don't want to get too big, I don't want to look like <u>that</u>."

I still have never really figured out what *that* is but I'm assuming, it's the 275-pound mass monster on the cover of *Men's Muscle & Fitness*, who is a few days off a win at the Mr. Master of the Universe Championship. He's standing ready for an on-site photo shoot with perfect lighting, a makeup artist, his muscles fully carbed-up and greased up with baby oil, hoisting enormous poundage with a bulging forehead vein and bicep vein to match. Him? Is that what <u>that</u> is? Don't worry, you won't.

Ladies, please note a few things. Because we are born female, at birth we were granted our own special set of natural hormones. We will never look like him in our natural state. Testosterone gives males the big, bulky, and swole appearance.

Women have estrogen. Lifting heavy weight whittles away at our body fat, giving us a lean and svelte appearance. That is our natural female biology.

For a woman to build lean muscle naturally, the body's environment has to be near perfect. I mean 90/10 percent perfect. At minimum, five days a week in the gym. At minimum, five meals per day, and eating every three to four hours without fail. Perfect hydration. Sleeping a minimum of eight hours each night, and if possible, a midday nap of sorts. Not to mention, supplementation, probiotics, and knowing how to hit your macronutrient ratios. My point is, this process is all consuming. I'm talking about Pure D 100% whole grain hard work, consistency, dedication, and discipline every day to achieve your best physique.

I can already hear the comments, "I have a friend with massive traps, it makes her look masculine." "Rian, your back is pretty wide, you said I wouldn't look like that." In bodybuilding, this is where you will start to hear the word *genetics* being thrown around and you will hear it often. "That guy has great genetics," or "Genetics won that category for her." In my family, we have professional athletes. All of us are genetically solid people. There are certain parts of my body that are more structurally sound and grow lean muscle quicker than others.

Genetically speaking, even as women, there are certain body parts that are dominant, bigger, or more developed and we don't get to decide. Genetics decides. Quads are a great example. You've seen those women who have great quads. It looks like they must spend five hours in the gym a day. They don't. They were born with great quads.

> Remember, even as women, we get our genetics from both mother and father.

Calves are another great example. The calf muscle is notorious for being genetically passed down from mom and dad. A small waist is genetic. You get what you get and then build a fantastic physique from there. Remember, even as women we get our genetics from both mother and father.

This is where a great coach enters the picture. A great coach will help you balance out your physique. Where you have massive traps, a great coach will assess your physique and help you develop your rear deltoid muscles, round out your shoulders, and develop your pectoral muscles. Now, when you look in the mirror, there is no body part that stands out as massive. You and your Coach have created and sculpted a balanced upper body. So, when your mind starts to play tricks on you – and it will – *You're getting too big, you're getting bulky, you don't want to look like that*, tell your mind, "Don't worry, you won't."

Chapter 6

NATURAL VS. NOT NATURAL

I don't want to be the bearer of bad news, but let's be clear, there are athletes at the top, elite levels of the sport who do use some kind of tool to enhance their on-stage appearance. What are they using? I don't know and it is not my place to know. It could be a cycle of testosterone, insulin, SARMS* or something as simple as a doctor prescribed diuretic.

No, I am not qualified to tell which steroid you should take to block specific hormones and exhibit others, but I am qualified to tell you that if you are considering becoming a bodybuilder and/or competing one day, begin with the end in mind. Determine whether or not competing is just a bucket list item – something to try once and move on – or if this something you want to continue doing competitively at the elite levels of the sport. Once you have made your decisions, then decide which organizations you wish to compete in. Some people know from the beginning, and some do not, and that's fine. I know you may have never thought of this concept. But again, I'm glad you're right here, right now, reading this book.

* Selective Androgen Receptor Modulators

I have studied bodybuilding my entire life. I was 36 years old and devastated when I showed my coach a picture of what I wanted to look like and she said, "Yeahhh, she's on something, she's too young and too big. That's not natural." I was shocked! What do you mean not natural? In my naivety, at thirty-six years old, I thought to myself, *well what else would you be if not natural?* And then my coach broke it down for me. What do you mean "blocking naturally occurring estrogen in my body?" Equine hormones, milliliters, and cc's! I wasn't ready for that conversation.

In that moment, I completely and utterly sympathized with nine-year-olds who find out that Santa isn't real. It is devastating, it really is. I had fallen for it. Just like everyone else, I had essentially fallen for "30 Days to Shredded Abs" and "12 Weeks to a Better You." I'd fallen for it in my own way.

After my coach cleared the weeds, she sat me down and we continued our conversation. After we got on the same page, we could now start laying a foundation for a proper client-coaching dynamic which means setting clear and realistic goals. I remember my coach looking me right in the eye and saying with full, unshakeable eye contact, "I train natural athletes, if that is the route you want to go down, (*that* being using performance enhancers), I am not the coach for you." Five years later we are still together.

The moral of this story really is that when you are looking at a magazine and following some influencer on Instagram—especially influencers at the top levels of the industry—yes, support them, admire them but remember to continue down *your* path, the path you have chosen for yourself. If you're in it for the long haul and want to go down the road of using performance enhancers, make sure your coach knows that from the beginning, especially if your coach only coaches natural athletes. It seems obvious, but you would be surprised.

> The moral of this story really is that when you are looking at a magazine and following some influencer on Instagram—especially influencers at the top levels of the industry—yes, support them, admire them but remember to continue down **your** path, the path you have chosen for yourself.

If your desire is to use performance enhancers, find a bodybuilding coach, or even better, a bodybuilding coach and a chemist, as these two professionals will be critical to your success. You need someone who can help you get on your cycle of performance enhancers, and get off of them without killing you.

Chapter 7

GO TO A SHOW

At this moment, if you have ever thought to yourself, *I want to do a show one day*, go to a show. Find a local show and go. At this point, it can be any show. Stay and watch from beginning to end, from prejudging through the awards ceremony at the night show. If you read the sentence before and don't know the difference between prejudging and the night show, that's perfect! It's time to go to a show.

Clear your entire Saturday, grab a notebook, your favorite pen, a gallon of water, and be prepared to take it all in. I also highly recommend that you pack your own food. One of the first things you will notice about the audience at a bodybuilding show is, aside from the fans, there are bodybuilders, trainers, and other fitness professionals present. Because of this, the typical concession options likely won't be available because bodybuilders, trainers, and fitness professionals won't eat them anyway. I have been at shows where the promoters didn't even pay to have the concession stands open. It simply wasn't worth the additional cost. Pack your meals, because after all, everyone else has their meals packed as well.

Now we can get to the good part!

Throughout the day, there are two things you should be prepared to hear and file away for your day on stage: from the judges, "Quarter turn to the right" and from the audience, "Ground up." You will hear these two phrases a lot. We will discuss the "ground up" concept a bit later in the book. Just below the stage there will a long table where a panel of five to eight, and sometimes ten, judges will be seated. Typically, the head judge will be sitting at the center of the table. You will not see him or her, as all of the judges are facing the stage, but you will hear the head judge's voices. Memorize the voice so you know exactly who is speaking and exactly who you should be listening for during comparison rounds.

Quarter turn to the right. Hear it. Breathe it. Dream it. Say it. Repeat it. Perfect it. *Quarter turn to the right.* There is one thing that shoots straight across all organizations, divisions, federations, countries, lands, races, body types, political opinions, and sports. All athletes quarter turn to the right.

I was in a posing class one day, and a fellow competitor said to our coach, "Why can't I turn to the left, the left side is my better side?" Coach answered, "Because all quarter turns are done to the right." That's the answer.

> There is one thing that shoots straight across all organizations, divisions, federations, countries, lands, races, body types, political opinions, and sports: all athletes quarter turn to the right.

I have actually witnessed, with my own eyes, a seasoned female physique competitor turn left. By seasoned, I mean at least 10 years of experience competing. The head judge was forgiving and repeated his call and waited for her to respond. Your nerves will get to you. It happens. But muscle memory speaks for itself. Quarter turn to the right.

Now is the time to grab the microscope and start doing your own research and development. I cannot tell you how many times I have been in a posing class standing next to a fellow athlete and she says, "I've never been to a show." Her fellow competitors crane their necks around to look at her in disbelief. She is more than half way into her 16-week process and has never even been to a show. That means she doesn't know what she is training for. Preparing to compete in a show isn't as simple as a Google search. You have to be in it, and your research must be done close-up. This is where the real due diligence comes in.

Once you have decided that you may compete one day, go to a show and don't blink. Every movement has meaning and every movement has purpose.

Chapter 8

MORNING SHOW VS. EVENING SHOW*

A bodybuilding show is the longest day ever; it is truly an all-day event. Plan for about 12 hours. When your fans go online to purchase a ticket, tickets will be listed "morning show only," "evening show only," or "all day." As mentioned earlier, this day is about you; so, the people that you want present for your day, your biggest fans, mom, dad, husband, boy/girlfriend, will need to purchase the "all day" ticket. For your supporters, have them purchase the "evening show only" tickets. Expect for them to pay $50 per ticket to come and support you. Don't make excuses for the price of admissions. Every fan club has a fee.

The Morning Show

The morning show is where prejudging is conducted. Prejudging is a long, arduous, and tedious process for the athletes, the judges, and the audience. Prejudging is a highly intriguing

---

* Some organizations such as Global Bodybuilding Organization GBO) and Naturally Fit Federation (NFF) are now doing what is called a straight through format and becoming quite proficient at it.

process, and this labor of love can last for hours. First, the head judge will convene the audience. He will take about 10 minutes to briefly explain the process of prejudging, which includes, how many minutes each athlete will have on stage to display his or her physique, how many poses to perform, which "walk" the athlete will be expected to perform, and introduce the expeditors. Lastly, stand for the anthem and then we are off to the races! The athletes from the first division are then called to the stage individually.

After each athlete has their individual time on stage, all of the athletes from the division are then brought out to the stage together and lined up in preparation to display their physiques in mandatory poses. Mandatory poses are unique in that this prevents competitor X from only showing her left side because it is more developed and better conditioned, giving her a leaner appearance. Or competitor Y from only posing himself in his most muscular pose. Having athletes show their physiques in mandatory poses, levels the playing field. Once the head judge begins calling mandatories, an athlete cannot hide anything. Mandatory poses are the same for everyone on the stage: front double bicep, side chest, side tricep, rear double bicep, and front abdominal and thigh. Or whatever the mandatory poses are for that division.*

When the athlete hears the call, they must immediately get into the mandatory pose the judge calls and hold it until the next call. Holding the pose gives the judges ample time to mark their scorecards and convene with their peers about who is showing themselves to be the gold standard at this moment in time. These are your comparison rounds.

---

*   Women's Bikini, Women's Figure, Wellness, and Men's Physique require a different style of mandatory posing.

Comparison rounds are done at prejudging and this is one of the most nail biting, uptight, on-edge, white knuckle, stressful moments your fans will *ever* experience. I say your fans because, you will be backstage. Unless your show happens to be in a performing arts center and has TV's in the bathroom areas, you won't be watching prejudging because, after all, you are the show!

You are getting finishing touches on your hair, tan, makeup, getting glued into your suit; and having someone from your fandom wait on your every need. Having been on both sides of prejudging, as a spectator and as a competitor, being a spectator is much more stressful. I mean, think about it. When is the last time you had the chance to watch a muscular and developed human physique on stage, in nothing but a sparkly cocktail napkin, then be compared to ten other humans also wearing sparkly cocktail napkins, moving their bodies into awkward poses called out by a stranger sitting at a table who is actually assigning a number score? Never. You can hear a pin drop in the room.

By sitting and observing as a spectator, you really start to understand how much work bodybuilding is. You begin to realize, yes, bodybuilding starts with five to six days a week in the gym and eating six meals a day. But it ends with this spectacular production of mandatory poses, comparison rounds, model walks, music, lights, camera, and action for which the athlete must practice and prepare. As a spectator, once you experience a few rounds and you actually begin to realize what is going on, you want all of the athletes to do well. After a few rounds, even as a first-time spectator, you begin to get an eye for what the judges are looking at. You start to pick up on the criteria. You actually start getting into the show. You will begin to have favorites. You begin to shuffle in your seat. You scoot to the edge of your seat a little bit, cross your arms, and maybe even reach for your glasses. I can hear you now talking to the person next to you, "His legs are bigger."

"Yea, but look at those shoulders. He has more definition; you can see the muscle more."

"I like her suit; she stands out more than the other girls."

What you are doing is exactly the same thing the judges are doing: critiquing. The judges have more specific criterion yes, but essentially the same thing. That is what makes prejudging so stressful, but really fun. All of this—the prejudging—happens during the morning show.

> What you are doing is exactly the same thing the judges are doing: critiquing. The judges have more specific criterion yes, but essentially the same thing.

The Evening Show

The evening show is insane! Crazy, insane energy. The size of the crowd doubles. The lights are brighter. The energy is higher. The evening show operates much like prejudging, except athletes in certain divisions will perform a routine. At the very end, athletes are awarded.* You will find that pretty much across all organizations, Men's Bodybuilding, Men's Classic Bodybuilding, and Women's Physique are the divisions that will perform a routine. Depending on the organization, Amateurs are given sixty seconds and Pros are given ninety seconds. The routine

---

* You may also hear the morning show and night show referred to as Prejudging and Awards Ceremony. This is because prejudging of the athletes' physiques occurs at the morning show. The judges reveal their scores at the evening show and that is when athletes are awarded.

performed during the evening show is counted in your scoring. However, remember, a total package is still required for a proper placement.

At both prejudging and the evening show you will have your stage shots taken. When you win, stage shots are the pictures you will want to keep forever. This is the best you have ever looked in your life! I'll have some tips for you later on.

Chapter 9

SHOULD I BRING MY KIDS?

I love seeing children at bodybuilding shows. It is an empowering environment, especially for kids who are old enough to understand how your behavior, eating style, personality, and energy level fluctuated during the months of your Prep. It's beneficial for them to see the final reward. Most kids will never get a glimpse of their parents at a more powerful moment: standing on stage, with all of the lights pointed at you, and they get to cheer for you. It doesn't get any better than that.

However, as a competitor you cannot be on parent duty. If you have children, be sure your significant other and family members are aware of the amount of time that he or she will be with the children without you. Your significant other or parent or whomever you've

> Most kids will never get a glimpse of their parents at a more powerful moment: standing on stage, with all the lights pointed at you, and they get to cheer for you. It doesn't get any better than that.

assigned to child duty has to be invested. On this day, there will be no, "Let's call Mommy and ask." There will be no, "Daddy will be here soon and you can ask him yourself."

On show day, the answer is, "Daddy is busy and we'll revisit this when we get home." Female competitors, you are wearing nails, dangly diamond earrings, high heels, tan, lots of oil, and an expensive and meticulously stoned suit. Fans and supporters alike must understand hands down that this is your day. This is not the normal you, you are a star! Aside from the fact your suit is glued on your body, so you will have to be waited on hand and foot, you should be waited on hand and foot anyway, because today is your day!

Children do not need to sit or be present at a bodybuilding show all day. For children, I recommend selecting the evening show, and I highly recommend a midday nap or whatever activity will allow them to be pleasant and enjoyable at 8:30 pm. That is when you finally get on stage, receive your hardware, and then go to IHOP® post-show with the other fifty athletes and their families, wait 45 minutes for a table and another 30 minutes for a stack of pancakes. Bring the iPad®, juice boxes, goldfish crackers, a friend, and the weighted blankets. Whatever your kid needs to behave, bring it.

They must understand that on this day, and this day only, you are not Mommy or Daddy – you can't be. You are a superstar, and all of your people know it.

Chapter 10

WOMEN'S PRO FIGURE AT THE DALLAS EUROPA

In other sports, athletes are on a pedestal, they are untouchable, and completely out of reach. After the game, you don't see them. They disappear behind the veil of stardom and are whisked off the court or off the field and down a tunnel into their cars to go do famous people things. That is not the case with bodybuilding. The athletes are accessible, all of your favorites are right there! You can touch them and talk to them. At its core, bodybuilding is the same for both the professional and the amateur athlete: discipline, heavy lifting and food. However, if you have an opportunity to witness the pros at work, you are in for a real treat. I had that opportunity at the Dallas Europa.

I had the pleasure of working the Dallas Europa with the Liquid Sun Rayz Texas Tanning Team. We partnered with Pro Tan to do the tanning, gluing, and glazing for the athletes. Backstage was electric! I had never seen so much chicken and rice, rice cakes, and sweet potatoes in one place. It was somehow reassuring, affirming. Somehow at that show, just being backstage, I felt that everything was alright with the world.

The Order of Events was per usual. Men's bodybuilding gets the crowd all riled up. But for whatever reason, at this particular show, the crowd was waiting for Women's Pro Figure. *They* were the stars of *this* show. Women's Figure is athletic, shiny, flashy, and above all else, classy. Women's Figure is pure joy! Backstage, all of the athletes are running around, grabbing a quick sip of water, running to the restroom, getting glued in again, tans touched up, and more. Backstage is super hype – bodies are moving everywhere!

Imagine a rave or the most hype house party you've ever been to. The music was loud. The DJ played every party song since 1975 and in perfect order. There was never a break or a lull in the music. The lights were flashing; there may have even been a disco ball. The host of the party planned all of the best cocktails; all of your favorite drinks are being served. I mean this party is lit! I forgot to mention the insane amount of cheering that went along with being at the *Dallas Europa*. I mean, all of your favorites are there. Everybody. The Europa Games is one of the who's who in bodybuilding events. Now replace the alcohol with rice cakes and honey, and it is a bodybuilding rave!

The moment Women's Pro Figure was called for gluing and glazing, the energy shifted. Let me back up for a second. What I mean by "called for gluing and glazing" is this: to ensure a smooth-running show, the backstage expeditor – typically dressed in all black – will yell out something like, "Women's Figure Class A, you are up next, line up for gluing and glazing." After hearing that announcement, athletes will come running, prancing, and tip toeing from just about every direction to line up for final touches on their stage ready presentation.

However, when the expeditor called for Women's Pro

Figure, the high, rave-like energy, from literally one minute ago changed. I mean, it was an immediate change. You could actually feel the energy shift in the room. The other athletes began moving out of the way. Something was about to happen.

I recall exactly what I was doing at the moment I heard the expeditor's call.

I had taken a knee to finish glazing one of the Men's 212 athletes. My head was down. The expeditor called Women's Pro Figure to the line. Unlike the nervous excitement, chatter, prancing, and short, choppy tiptoeing when the previous amateur female divisions were called, the sound of certainty entered the room. The way the Women's Pro Figure athletes' heels hit the ground sounded different. The spacing between their steps was longer. The time it took their heels to hit the ground was longer. The air changed. I get chills thinking about it. And mind you, I am taking all of this in with my head down. In the moment, I couldn't look up, I was working with another athlete, but I was 100% sure of what was going on around me. I could hear the strut of confidence entering the room.

The energy in the entire convention center shifted from this high rave-like intensity to serious just by the cadence of their steps.

> They carried a confidence that didn't need words.

Their stride. I remember someone saying, "The stallions are here." Stone cold serious, elegant, strong and silent. Yes. The stallions had arrived. That is exactly what they were—the stars of the show. The quiet before the storm. They didn't say a word and that is what I noticed first. They carried a confidence that did not need words.

I was immediately taken by how serious they were. Not

mean, just serious. They were 100% focused on performing at 100% capacity. Even how they stood while they were being glued and glazed was different. It was professional. Amateurs will look at their bodies and watch every little thing you do. Amateurs come back and ask questions such as, "Can you get right here; can you rub right there?" The Figure Pros did not ask questions. They did not talk to each other or us. They stood and looked straight ahead. They never looked down while we were working, but they knew exactly which body part was being glazed, as they would flex at just the right moment.

When the work was done, they offered a polite thank you, swung their hair, and strutted off.

Have you ever been around someone who made you behave differently? Like in a good way, just better? Well, that is Women's Pro Figure. Elegant, serious, and focused. I didn't even think of asking a question or even wasting my words by saying "Good luck," I just worked.

Everything I needed to know about professional behavior, I learned from the Women's Pro Figure athletes at the Dallas Europa. They were a thing of beauty.

Chapter 11

THE RIGHT SUIT

Your show day suit will amount to just about a three triangular cocktail napkins with three holes in it: one hole for your head and two holes for your legs. Because of this, finding the right suit may be one of the most panic-inducing and stressful, yet exciting aspects of your competition prep!

As mentioned in the chapter *It's Expensive!* earlier, you will need to send your designer or rental company a deposit. In the midst of everything in your life, the deposit kind of pops up out of nowhere. Obviously, I knew I needed to purchase a suit, but there will be a point in your prep where you really feel the clock ticking. One day, *I need to order suit swatches* was in my subconscious, and the next day my designer sent me a Venmo. Of course, that is not what really happened, but the reality is that you will get to a point in prep when life starts moving really fast. You can guarantee your suit maker is cutting and stoning suits for at least fifty other girls, trust me on this. You want your suit to arrive on time for a fitting, and, if necessary, return to sender if any adjustments need to be made.

Just before you enter prep, start asking around for referrals for professional competition suit designers. By the time you enter prep, you will want to have a suit designer narrowed down. Send an email to connect well in advance, because a fabulous designer will be booked for several shows, months in advance, so you will want to get on your designer's calendar as soon as possible.

Regarding picking the right suit, I have received two of the best pieces of advice.

The first piece of advice comes from 10x Ms. Olympia Iris Kyle:

"Once you find your color, stick with it.
Don't keep switching colors."

In this specific segment of the fitness industry, you will hear the word "package" used over and over. During athlete interviews, you'll hear, "This year I've got the total package, next year I'm bringing a better package, this season my package is complete," etc. The right suit is a part of the total package you are presenting to the judges for scoring. To use the metaphor of wrapping paper: your suit is the wrapping paper on a perfect gift and on show day, that gift is you!

I had a seamless experience with Decked in Diamonds by George Ann Lazarou.

On a particular Tuesday, scrolling Facebook, alas! I saw a suit on a competitor that I absolutely adored. I took a screenshot and sent George Ann a message that said, "Can we do something like this?"

She responded later that afternoon affirming the suit and asked if I had any colors in mind. I decided to go with shades of green. About ten days later, via USPS, I received about fifteen cloth swatches of different shades of green, all stapled to piece of paper all labeled with incredibly creative names. Some of the color swatches were overlaid with pattern, some swatches were holographic, and others were snakeskin patterned, yet all still green. My little mind hadn't hoped or dreamed of much more than a shade of stoplight green, so when I opened the envelope and I saw the variations not only in color, but patterning and texture, I was beyond shocked.

My suit designer took what I said and put her creative professional spin on it. She took my original vision to another level. You will hear me say repetitiously, "Use the competition professionals." There is a difference between a person who can sew on a button and person who can take initial measurements on a still changing body, and then cut, design, stone, and hook attachments on a suit that will fit like a glove a few weeks after receiving it.

I took my measurements using a measuring tape, wrote them on a sticky note and sent the picture of the sticky note to the designer via a Facebook message. A few days later, she reached out and sent me a few pictures of options for the diamond neck and hip attachments, I responded with my choices, and she went back to work.

The initial communication should go something like this. (You will definitely want to stroke the designer's ego a little bit.)

"I saw a suit you made on a competitor at Ultimate Muscle Extravaganza. Her picture was on Instagram." Tell the designer what exactly you liked about that suit. And then ask, "Do you think you could do something like that for me? I'm thinking of going with a shade of orange."

Allow the professional designer take it from there and submit to her expertise.

I personally know girls who have spent hours and hours of unnecessary brain power on "finding someone" to make a suit for them. Does this someone you are finding know that a Women's Bikini competitor and Women's Physique competitor do not wear the same style competition suit? I know your best friend's mother made the two of you matching swimsuits the summer before 7th grade, but she may not be the ideal candidate for this job.

The professional will tell you things like, *there isn't enough contrast between your skin color and the suit or the stones you've picked won't really pick up the light like you think they will.* Your best friends' mother will not. You can spend hours, and I mean hours, of phone calls to your homegirls, and seventy-five text messages to six people whose opinions don't even matter; because the fact of the matter is that on show day, the only opinions that really matter are the judges: center, left, and right.

Additionally, your suit designer should not need to send you every color known to man, because every color known to man is not going to look good on your complexion. I would never need to ask my suit maker for anything in the yellow, orange or light pink family. I'm already that color! So, keep it focused. Tell your suit designer what you want and allow her to throw all of her creative talent and design into your perfect suit.

As you are selecting your suit color, in the back of your mind don't forget about your competition spray tan. Yes, you are picking a color that compliments your current skin tone, but don't forget that on show day you will be two to three shades darker than your current skin tone, and that matters! That is where I went wrong, and it is actually something that I had not even thought of until it was too late. Just before I stepped on stage, I took one final look at myself. At that moment I realized two things: my suit was still as beautiful as the moment I first pulled it out of the 5" x 8" puffy mailing envelope. It still shined, glimmered, glistened, and blinged just as planned, but now against my new skin tone, with three coats of tan, the suit color did not pop as much as it did without the tan. Adding tan to my skin brought my skin tone and the color of the suit closer together in shade. File this information away for later.

The second piece of advice came from my coach Melanie Daly:

"Buy your suit."

Competition suit rentals have become much more popular in the recent years. A top-notch suit rental company will take suits off of the market to fix any errors. However, I've been a witness to an athlete wearing a rented suit with stretched seams. Apparently the rental company told her, "You are the last athlete to wear it before it goes back to the shop for repairs." And she was okay with it! This falls into the *you don't know what you don't know* category. She didn't know that wasn't okay. If you do decide to rent your suit, inspect it carefully: stitching at the seams, hooks, neck and hip attachments, seat of the suit, and elastic around the cups and bikini bottoms. There may be someone on the planet that has the exact same measurements as you do, but the chances of finding that person may literally be one in a million. The bikini top and bottom may show the same measurements on paper, but that does not mean it will fit your body perfectly.

A personal training client of mine asked me, "Why would someone rent a suit?"

A friend of mine loves scheduling her shows back to back. I mean why not, you already look great, so stay in the process

> The first piece of advice: **"Once you find your color, stick with it. Don't keep switching colors."** The second piece of advice: **"Buy your suit."**

for another 7 days. Let's say she registers for two shows in the same organization. One show on Saturday, October 25th and Saturday, November 1st, and both shows are in the same organization. She is an experienced competitor and she knows she will be in front of the same judges; therefore, she definitely wants to compete in two different suits. The October 25th show is a smaller show, at a smaller venue, with fewer athletes registered. She decides to rent her suit. However, the November 1st show has over two hundred athletes registered. All along, in the back of her mind, she knew the extra week of training and dieting would make a difference in her physique. On November 1st, she chooses to use a custom competition suit. This is just an example of one athlete's thought process as she approaches the decision to buy versus rent.

The first and most obvious con to renting a suit is that someone else has already worn it. The second con is that the suit is not custom. Even if you've never competed before, you know how little material covers the body. You need all of your material and every stitch needs to be perfect. However, there are some rental companies out there that deliver an extremely high-quality product. There are companies that absolutely do their due diligence in regards to sanitizing, stain and glue removal, and restitching seams.

> Try on your suit so you know exactly where you

need hair removal. Do not guess. Wax prior to your show to ensure there is no irritation.

Thinking back to the day I received those swatches, having them in my possession made show day real. The day was coming! When you receive your swatches, be prepared to drop $300 for your deposit, step back, and prepare to be amazed.

The bottom line is this: find your color and stick with it, contrasting and complementary color choice matters, if you are able to spend the money, buy your suit and whether you buy or rent, always use a reputable competition suit professional.

I highly recommend using Decked in Diamonds by GeorgeAnn Lazarou – her process was truly impressive.

Contact your suit maker and ask if she would be willing to make a few enhancements to your current suit. Here a few tips on how to change the appearance of your suit. It's worth the ask.
- **Add more stones; clear or colored.**
- **Switch out your neck and hip attachments.**
- **Change the style of your posing heels.**
- **Add stoning to your current posing heels.**

Divisions are becoming much more scrupulous about how much or little coverage is allowed. Don't mess around with this. Every show has an athlete check-in, and one of your check-ins could very well be a stop at the judge's table for a suit inspection. They are checking for coverage. Don't gamble! Remember reading the chapter *It's Expensive!* You will have literally thrown your money down the drain by coming in with a suit that does not clear inspections. I recommend you don't play that game with a judge, especially the female judges.

Chapter 12

THE STAGE

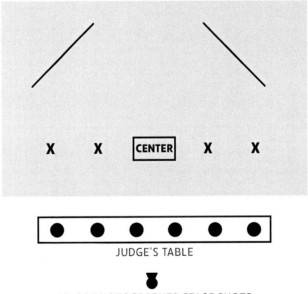

JUDGE'S TABLE

STAGE PHOTOGRAPHER STAGE SHOTS

The first rule of entering the stage is this: if you can see the audience, the judges can see you.

At most venues, you will climb a short flight of steps that are level to and fused against the side of the stage. Backstage, the expeditor will line you up in the order that the judges will call you to enter the stage. As you ascend the staircase, know that the moment you are able to see the audience, the judges can see you. That means smile – really smile – and hold it. Just because you are not on stage performing your model walk or t-walk, know that, the performance has begun! By the time you get to the top step, you should be just about ready to lock and load.

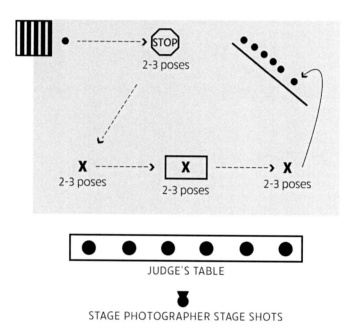

JUDGE'S TABLE

STAGE PHOTOGRAPHER STAGE SHOTS

Most any stage you walk onto will have at least three or four x's taped to the floor and one square or rectangle taped to the floor center stage. There will also be at least one diagonal line at the rear of the stage. Depending on the number of athletes registered for the show, there may be two lines, one on each side of the stage. Tape helps the expeditors, as well as the athletes mark their stops on stage. When you arrive at the venue, I highly recommend you not only look at the stage, but also walk it. While you are walking the stage, you are looking for places where tape could lift from the stage. Inevitably, at your first show, the stage will be carpeted, and the tape will lift off the carpet. What that means for you as an athlete is, if you are competing in a division that wears heels, the bottom of your shoes will stick to the tape. While you are practicing your quarter turns, file this bit of information away. You will quickly understand why perfect practice of your quarter turns and muscle memory is crucial. At some point in your career, tape will be public enemy number one! Your coach will be able to gather more information from the show promoter about which side of the stage athletes will enter from. In case you forget, you will likely be informed again at the athlete's meeting.

Just before the announcer calls your name, confirm with the expeditor which "walk" you will be performing. Engage your muscles, your smile, and go! It's game on baby! No matter which walk you have been instructed to do, at each taped x you will stop and hit the style pose your division calls for. At every x , pose in slow motion. If you feel like, *I've been standing here holding this pose forever,* it is the perfect amount of time. Here is the script that goes through my head: *Walk to the X. Stop. Set feet. Contract all muscles. Smile. Count 3 seconds. 1-2-3. Move.* Use this script at each x. It's a lot, I know; but this script will keep you slow and deliberate.* One of the most important takeaways is this: performing the t-walk or model walk is the only time you will be on stage by yourself the entire day, and it is a short time. It is crucial to display everything you have, your entire package, as flawlessly as you are able, the very first time.

As you are performing on stage, don't forget the most

---

* For Divisions like Women's Bikini, where the greatest number of athletes are registered, the judges will call competitors' names quickly. As soon as you arrive at the center stage box, the announcer is calling the next Athletes name. Keep this in mind, but don't get flustered! Go ahead and do whatever you and your coach practiced, while simultaneously using discretion, knowing the next athlete is right behind you and expecting you to move along.

important stop: the taped square. Stand directly in the middle of that square and smile – because that is where the photographer will capture your stage shots!

For Divisions like Women's Bikini, where the greatest number of athletes are registered, the judges will call competitors names quickly. Keep this in mind, but don't get flustered!

Chapter 13

KNOW THE CRITERIA FOR YOUR DIVISION

There are several new divisions opening up. New organizations are growing, some regionally and others internationally. Global Bodybuilding Organization (GBO) is a great example of this, they are growing like wildfire! They are adding more shows regionally, nationally, and internationally.

After you determine which organization you will compete in, the next thing you and your coach will need to do is determine which qualities your physique already possesses thanks to genetics, meaning what strengths your physique already has. Afterwards, your coach will design your training to balance out or develop the other areas of your physique, so that you'll be competitive in your division. The moment you enter the gym with your new training plan is the moment you need to know the criteria for your division.

When I think about the concept of knowing the criteria for your division, I automatically think about research! In my mind, knowing the criteria for your division includes knowing general information about the organization you're competing in, the specific physical requirements of the division, which style competition suit is regulation, accessory selection, what style heels athletes are wearing this season, and mandatory poses. That criteria also includes people—the other athletes that compete in your division, at your level.

Stay On Your Level

I strongly believe other athletes in your division are your blueprint, so to speak.

I have observed novice competitors measuring the progress of their physique against well-seasoned competitors in the Pro Divisions. I am not talking about your garden variety hero worship here. I have physiques that I have constantly studied and still do—Latorya Watts, Lenda Murray, Iris Kyle, and Kai Greene. I've spent my share of hours in front of the computer in awe. I am not talking about simply having a favorite competitor and aspiring to be similar to them based on qualities of their physique or characteristics that you admire. I'm talking about looking at a well-seasoned pro and comparing your physique with a "Why don't I have that yet?" or "I should look like that already!" perspective and then judging yourself negatively based on that. I cannot nor should I ever measure my still near-novice physique against seasoned (I'm talking well-seasoned, muscles-have-been-in-the-slow-cooker-for-years) athlete! You're not being fair to yourself, stay on your level.

It is your responsibility, however, to learn about the athletes in your region, area, and local gyms that intend to compete in your division. Go to the organization's website. If the show was streamed, watch the show from the previous year and find the winners. Study the physiques of the first, second, and third place winner. They are standing right next to each other and you can clearly see what the judges awarded, and then you can get to work. For me, I studied pictures and knew I had to get to work on my quad sweep. Become a student of your division by learning the criteria and nuances. Your great-

> I cannot, nor should I ever, measure my still near novice physique against a seasoned (I'm talking well-seasoned, muscles-have-been-in-the-slow-cooker-for-years) athlete! You're not being fair to your-self, stay on your level.

est competition likely isn't a pro athlete that advanced to the 2021 Ms. Solar System of the Entire Universe contest – it's probably the girl in the next town over at Planet Fitness that works out, facing the wall, in a hoodie and sweatpants that nobody even pays attention to! It's her! Not the current 2021 reigning Ms. Solar System Champ!

The Pretty Boys

This observation has been made typically among male competitors, especially if they have a borderline physique. Men's Classic Physique and Men's Physique are two divisions that are easy to pick on because the division names are so similar, and can cause some confusion. An athlete could absolutely register and compete in both Men's Classic Physique and Men's Physique, but because he didn't know the criteria for his divisions and only heard the word "physique" in the name, he assumed the divisions are the same. These two divisions are not the same. The posing trunks are not the same, and neither are the poses.

Men's Physique is a different look than Men's Classic

Physique. This is important because the athlete would have to study the criteria for both divisions.

Men's Physique is the pretty boy category. Part of the criteria for competing in Men's Physique is being pretty. Let's say for example you register for both Men's Classic Physique and Men's Physique. You have to be able to make that switch! You have to be able to show a massive, forceful, strong, powerful hulking physique that takes up tons of space on stage! And then almost immediately, hurry off stage and transform completely and return to the stage as a peacock.

It is the same body, but using posing and your trunks, you actually have to transform into two different people.

Attention to detail is a part of knowing the criteria for your division. Being pretty is a part of the total package you are presenting. I find some of my guys struggle with this part the most. I completely understand if you are not a pretty boy in your regular life, but today is different.

I've witnessed athletes not being able to make the switch. I remember a male competitor with an incredible physique—I mean a chiseled, spectacular Adonis. Truly impressive! He was also wearing some baggy, gray, extra-large Walmart swim trunks he found at the last minute. Something you would see on a regular guy, drinking a regular beer, on a regular beach, in a regular town. I was shocked! He didn't study the criteria for his division. Yes, he knew how to use posing to adapt his physique to two divisions, but personality wise he was not able to turn on his pretty boy charm.

Buying from a specialty shop* is a little trick that ensures no

---

* If you are not already following Chula Wear @chulastylz_ on Instagram, you absolutely should be. Chula Wear is the ultimate definition of specialty!

one else will have on your shorts. There is nothing like standing in line waiting to walk the steps to the stage and seeing two other guys wearing your shorts. I'll say it again and again: at the end of the day, this sport is subjective. As an audience spectator, the first thing we will see is two guys that have the same shorts on. If we see it, you can bet your Pro Card, the judges see it too.

For all things pretty, find a specialty shop. Go to a reputable source and figure out where the peacocks buy their swim trunks? You have to. You must try them on and you have to spend time in the mirror. This is the time to know, does this color look good on me, *do these make my butt look big*?

"I always suggested to my Athletes doing a spray tan rehearsal 4-6 weeks out. This allows the tan lay for a week or so and then to come off completely. While you've got your spray tan on, try several different pairs and colors trunks to be sure there is enough contrast between your tanned skin tone and the color of the shorts. It might be worth a dry run on skin prep and exfoliation the week before. The other piece of advice is to have a one hour tailor on hand. If you are travelling for your show, call ahead and be sure there is a one hour tailor in the city or closeby. Guys make sure the waistline is not too loose or too tight. Being in prep, my waist shrunk the most the last 2 weeks. Also, always bring backup trunks even for guys."

—Matt Storm, GBO Pro Men's Beach Body Athlete, GBO Certified Judge, GBO Arizona/California State Director, Storm Classic/Global Open/Global Invitational Promoter

Jewelry

In the female categories, each division has a slightly different style of jewelry. It is your responsibility as the athlete to know which style is most popular for your category. Let's use Women's Physique as our example. At minimum, a Women's Physique competitor will want to wear one thick diamond studded bracelet on each wrist and one thick diamond ring on either the left or right forefinger. Any additional rings are personal choice. Typically, there is no jewelry around the neck, as your suit will have blinged out attachments around the neck and shoulder. You will, however, need to find earrings that suit you. I wore diamond studs; they suited me. Next time, I will definitely go bigger. Remember that this is a show! It is a competition. Pick jewelry that is flattering, yet allows you to stand out from the girl next to you.

Register for the categories in your Division

This is a part of knowing the criteria for your Division. Think of it as the equivalent of LeBron James playing a scrimmage game with his teammates. If you've studied practically anything, you know the difference between theoretical knowledge and practical application. Because bodybuilding is a solo sport, registering for as many categories as possible is our scrimmage, except we scrimmage with ourselves. The second and third time you set foot on stage you start to ooze confidence, and it shows! More stage time equals more comfort, comfort equals confidence, and confidence can get you a closer to the top on the scorecard. You also increase your chances of coming home with some hardware and that's the equivalent of winning a championship game!

Pay the fees to register for every category available to you. You will be glad you did.

Become a student of the game. Knowing the criteria for your division is everything you are already doing: hours in the gym, reading books, sitting in discussions with seasoned athletes, watching hours and hours of film, and attending live shows. This is how you perfect your craft.

Chapter 14

POSING YOUR PHYSIQUE

Posing your physique is the key element to success on stage. It helps you display your physique in its most favorable form. Posing allows you to properly display your physique and ensures you stand out in your comparison rounds. If you are a novice competitor, ideally you want to begin posing about one year prior to stepping on stage. I started learning to pose my physique in February, and did not compete until the following July. Posing helps you stand confidently in your body and showcase the strengths of your physique. It is not enough just to sweat and grunt in the gym. An athlete can have the most beautiful round delts on the planet, but if she does not know how to get them to "pop"…well, that's unfortunate. Learning how to pose your physique is a critical piece of the bodybuilding craft.

Remember Competitor X from a few chapters ago? The one who said, "My left side is my better side, so why can't I turn left?" This is where learning how to pose your physique enters our world. We all have imbalances. The left side of my upper body is bigger and more muscularly developed than the right. The right side of my lower body is better developed than the left. This imbalance was created from an injury about 15 years ago. What is interesting is that the injury never showed itself until I started lifting. Once my body leaned out and I learned how to hold my frame and contract my muscles properly, the imbalance was barely noticeable. I had to learn to squeeze the right bicep harder and rotate my wrist backwards a tenth of inch further on the right than the left. I had to learn how "dig" my big toe in the ground harder on the left side so the muscles of the leg would pop equally the same as the right. The dig allows the calf muscle to pop, and lifts and separates the glutes from the hamstring, and gives you enough stability to flex and "split" your quads well for the judges to see.

"Digging" the toes into the ground is the concept of "ground up" that you hear from the audience. A phenomenal posing or presentation coach will teach you that all of your posing movements and muscle contractions begin from the ground. Setting yourself from the "ground up" means flexing your muscles from the floor: squeeze toes, especially the big toe into the ground or into your heels. Next flex the calves, hamstrings, glutes, and quads, then draw your entire core to the center and put a slight arch in the lower back.

Next is the famous and beautiful lat flare. Flaring the lats simultaneously flexes the entire back, chest and shoulders. Finally, after the lats have been flared, push your pecs upwards and out into your arms pits at the same time. In one motion, the lat flare basically flexes the entire upper body. Last but not least, twist* and smile. Generally, this is the order for *hitting your quarter turn* and then *setting yourself from the ground up*. There are, of course, some variations to this order, especially in Women's

---

* Depending on the pose you are getting into. Front and Rear poses do not require a twist in the core.

Bikini, but this pretty much nails it and each coach will have his or her own styling tips and techniques. What posing will teach you is that the devil is in the details.

So, let's run through this together. Once you hit your quarter turn (and by hit your quarter turn, I mean pivot), set yourself from the ground up. Squeeze your toes into the ground. This creates a chain reaction of muscle flexion through the calves, into the hamstrings and glutes, and quads. Pull the entire core in and flare your lats while simultaneously pushing the chest upwards towards the sky and outwards under the armpits, and depending on the pose, twist, drop the chin a bit and smile.

All of this is supposed to appear effortless.

Ladies, remember those shoes I mentioned back in the chapter called *It's Expensive?* Start shopping now for your shoes. All of the above must be done in heels under extremely hot stage lights. I can hear it now, "I walk in heels all the time, my Jimmy Choo™s are so comfortable, I can run in them. I'll be fine." When you start your posing class, order your shoes. You should be practicing your posing in the same shoes you plan to wear on stage. Walk in your shoes daily. Wash the dishes, vacuum the floor in them, mow the lawn in them. Go to the grocery store. You may get a few funny looks, but it's fun! Only a phenomenal coach will explain to you how to achieve all of this; how to pose your body and even use the bling on your nails to attract attention.

By the time you get to the stage six months to a year from now, your posing should be like running a simple elementary school drill. Both your mandatory poses and, if you have one, your evening show posing routine should be embedded into your muscle spindles. It should be like knowing your ABCs. You learned them so long ago, you don't remember life without them. Your posing routine should be like this to you. You know it so well; you can't remember a time in your life when you did not know it. Embed it!

Your posing routine should be like knowing your ABCs. You learned them so long ago, you don't remember life without them.

Chapter 15

MANDATORY POSES

Each division of bodybuilding has its own mandatory poses. You have been studying and watching film, so you know what your organization and division will require of you. The head judge will determine how many Athletes he or she wants to compare at the same time. Most often, the judge will call five or six competitors to stand center stage.

"Front double bicep. Relax. Favorite side chest. Relax. Best side tricep. Relax. Rear double bicep. Relax. Front abdominal and thigh. Thank you, please exit the stage."

Generally, that will be the call you are listening for. Remember, there will be variations between the male and female categories. For example, Men's Classic Bodybuilding will hit all of the above mandatory poses, as well as most muscular and possibly favorite classic pose. Even still, you will see the foundational mandatory poses first, with a few additions based on their specific category.

Women's Physique and Women's Bikini are both female categories, but the posing criterion for each category is different. For example, front double bicep is a mandatory Women's

Physique pose, however, you will not see Bikini athletes "hitting" the front double bicep. It just wouldn't be right.* Bikini athletes will still perform their version of quarter turns but the expectation for how the Bikini athlete performs the mandatory pose is different. In some Organizations, Women's Bikini will be asked to face rear, walk to the back curtain, face front, walk forward. No flexing or separation between muscle groups. The judges are looking for a softer, rounder shape, with muscle, but not too much muscle, presented with poise, grace, and a beautiful skin tone, all at the same time! That's hard.

At this point in your learning, you can begin practicing your mandatory poses on your own. Here's a tip on how to practice on your own: on a sheet of paper, write down the phrase above: "Front double bicep. Relax. Favorite side chest. Relax. Best side tricep. Relax. Rear double bicep. Relax. Front abdominal and thigh."** Give this sheet to a friend. Ask your friend to say "Front double bicep," and pause thirty seconds. In these thirty seconds you are to hold your body in the front double bicep position. Repeat the same sequence all the way to the end. I recommend repeating this sequence three times post-workout, and then rest for the day. We would say something like, "Let's run through your mandatories." Begin with once a week, then twice, then three times a week. As you participate in this repetitive activity, you are training your mind to become accustomed to hearing your poses called out in this order. Even if you are a bikini athlete, I recommend you give it a go. The reason being, even though these poses are not your mandatories, going through them will teach you how to contract your muscles and keep

---

*   Now in a pose down, you might see anything.
**   For Women's Bikini and Men's Physique divisions, research the language for your division and follow the same instructions.

them contracted. Even though the bikini athletes make their posing look effortless, believe me, every single muscle is contracted!

In selecting your coach, you must be able to articulate which division you are considering so you and your coach can be on the same page regarding which mandatory poses you should be practicing. Three to four weeks out from your show and as your body starts to lean out, your coach will continue to finesse adjustments and final touches. What I mean by that is, a pose that looked absolutely amazing on your physique five weeks ago, may not look so good as you lean out; now there may be an even better pose that showcases the strengths of your physique. Constant adjustment is necessary because your body is changing up to and through the day of the show.

Once you are invested in the prep process, your coach will take what you have already committed to memory and connect it to your muscles. Your posing coach will then actually teach you how to flex, contract, hold, and make yourself look bigger, fuller, trimmer, leaner, create a better shoulder to hip ratio, or whatever the look is for your division. Going into your first posing class knowing at least the mandatory poses for your division puts you a step ahead. Your coach will take it from there.

Novice Tip: To this day, the first thing I do in the morning is start my shower water. While the water is warming up, I run through my mandatory poses. It has become a habit. Running through my mandatory poses is my form of morning stretching. Plus, I'm vain. I like to make sure my muscles are still there!

Chapter 16

COMPARISON ROUNDS

During comparison rounds, you will, exactly as the title indicates, be compared.

At this point in the competition, every aspect of your physique and presentation is now being critiqued by the judges. This is where you will hear all of fandom yelling things like, "Hit it from the ground up!" and "Make the judges work!" "Make the judges work" is my favorite phrase because there's so much truth in it.

Every athlete on the stage has done the grunt work in the gym, they've all been through a grueling prep, but now it's show time. It's time to show the judges who deserves to win awards. It's time to show the judges what you've got. "Make the judges work" means the competition is so stiff that the judges have to work hard to make the right decision. You will see the most movement during the comparison rounds. So, let's get down to it.

Athletes will run through their comparison rounds at least three times: muscle size/development, muscle symmetry, and conditioning.

Muscle Size/Development

Muscle development is a question of time. How much time has been spent developing your physique? How much time have you spent stripping down muscle fibers and how much time have you given your muscles to repair? How much time has been spent putting good, quality muscle on your frame? How developed are your muscles compared to the competitor next to you? Muscle development applies to every athlete from Women's Bikini to Men's Heavyweight Bodybuilding. Have your muscles been developed appropriately for your category?

Muscle Symmetry

Symmetry is balance. Balance means a symmetrically developed muscular physique from top to bottom, left to right, and front to back. Imagine the guy that skips leg day; he is an example of not being symmetrical. He is not balanced top to bottom. Picture the girl in the gym who works her glutes only. She's not symmetrical anywhere! Now, there will be certain aspects of your physique that are naturally not symmetrical. Using myself as an example, the entire left side of my upper body is bigger than the right. My right side is lagging; it just grows along at its own pace. As an athlete, look at your body but don't obsess. Your coach is able to be more objective, but you look too, as you will always have the inside intel on yourself first. Also, posing done right will ensure that you display muscle symmetry even if the symmetry is not quite there.

Conditioning

Conditioning is your cardio, plain and simple. During your prep, how tight and lean were you able to get your body? Your coach will know how lean you need to be to showcase a competitive physique in your division. Each division, male and female, requires a different level of leanness. A Women's Bikini does not necessarily need to be quite as lean as a Women's Physique competitor. A phenomenal coach will know. Knowing how lean you should be for your division is the most critical piece of information for which you are paying a coach.

Comparison rounds will happen for the first time during prejudging at the morning show and again during the evening show. It is possible that the judges will run athletes through comparison rounds much more rigorously during the morning show than during the evening show. Down in Beaumont, the competition in Women's Physique was so stiff, the judges ran through comparison rounds eight times. Eight. So, remember, three is the minimum. The judges needed five more rounds of comparisons and moving athletes around, before they were satisfied with their scorecards.

As mentioned before, during comparison rounds, you will see a lot of movement. During this time judges are making their most professional subjective critiques of the athletes. In order to do this, judges must move the athletes around. Remember, the judges are sitting at a long rectangle table, 10-20 feet long. If as a judge I am sitting on the far right of the table, I am unable to give the athlete on the far left of the stage a fair and accurate critique. The judge simply cannot see well enough to score accurately and fairly.

In order for the judges to get the most subjective view of all of the athletes, you will hear the head judge start calling out numbers.

"Number 5 switch places with #14. Thank you. And #15 switch places with #25. Ladies, spread out. Give each other some room. Alright, let's go again. Front double bicep. Relax. Favorite side chest. Relax." And so on.

The head judge will continue calling out mandatory poses as outlined in the previous chapter, mandatory poses. The head judge will continue switching and moving athletes around as many times as necessary until all of the judges are satisfied with their critiques and have submitted their scoring for the score cards.

Remember that diagonal line referred to in the chapter called *The Stage?* Depending on the number of athletes in the class, the judge will call them to center stage. The athletes will be standing on the diagonal line in their relaxed pose, waiting to be called out. I promise you; you will not be able to hear anything. What you will do is keep your eyes fixed on the expeditor.

The head judge will say something like this, "Numbers 56, 27, 13, 12, 40, and 49 to the center please." The Expeditor will pull you to your assigned x on the stage. At this point, I strongly recommend, immediately setting yourself in your front relaxed pose. Immediately. Remember, if you are on stage, you are being judged. Period. This is a performance. I cannot stress this enough. Once the expeditor places you, right away hit your front pose. Hitting your front pose immediately says to the judges, "Look at me, I'm confident, professional and ready."

After the Judges are satisfied, you will hear, "Thank you and see you tonight."

It's over.

After the judges are satisfied, you will hear, "Thank you and see you tonight."
It's over.

Chapter 17

HOW TO WIN YOUR CLASS, AND THEN OVERALL

Divisions will often be divided into classes. If a show has one hundred competitors registered for one division, it is virtually impossible for all 100 athletes to be on the stage at the same time. There's just no way, as it is visually overwhelming for everyone. Spectators and fans won't know who to look at! The expeditors will spend most of their time searching for the competitors' numbers. The stage isn't big enough, and think of the judges' eyes! There is a point in the day where everyone starts to look the same. Bodybuilding is already a subjective sport, so anything that makes the athletes look the same is an absolute negative.

In an effort to prevent a division from becoming a blinged-out meat market, on your initial registration you are asked for your height. This allows the show promoters to begin tallying an accurate athlete count, and then sort athletes into classes to prepare for a smoother running show.

Stop for a moment and think about why athletes would be divided into classes. It is overwhelmingly obvious when you have an athlete that is 5'4" standing next to an athlete who is

6'5." The taller athlete will draw more attention, as the eye auto-matically pulls toward the taller athlete. Even if the taller ath-lete is less conditioned, less symmetrical and less developed, it never fails: the eye picks up on height. Separating and judging by height is another way to keep the sport fair during compar-ison rounds.

A practical example of the reason why athletes are separated by height is The Rock and Kevin Hart. Imagine the two of them standing next to each other. It is quite obvious that both actors take bodybuilding and fitness seriously. Kevin Hart has incred-ibly developed and conditioned muscle, meaning he appears leaner by having less body fat than The Rock. Kevin Hart is also nearly perfect in symmetry. Yet the average human is still drool-ing over The Rock. And for what? He is massive. He is bigger. That's how the average eye has been trained—big is good. Small is bad. People think bigger is better. In bodybuilding, that is not necessarily true.

You can spot a first-time audience member by comments like, "He's bigger, why didn't he win. She should've won because her legs are bigger." I shake my head. Novices. The only thing that matters is muscle development, symmetry, and conditioning.

We will use Women's Bikini* as our example, because Bikini typically has the largest number of athletes, so the explanation and understanding of how to win your class, and then overall, is a bit clearer.

---

* This example is a highly simplified example. But it gives you a basic foundation in the concept of how to win your class and overall. Take this example and apply it across your registered division, categories, and classes. Additionally, some shows are two day shows. If you win the overall on the first day, you may be in the running for your Pro card on day two. Just know that, at the end of the day, how athletes will be awarded is decided by the organization and show promoters.

Your announcer will say, "We are going start our judging with Women's Bikini Novice Class A."

Our judges' roster will read:

Novice Class A 5'0" – 5'4"
Jordan Jamison
Mikaela Marcos
Nicola Nahuma
Monica Mejia
Alexis Combs
Marquette Richey
Ryker Roland

Novice Class B 5'5" – 5'10"
Rori Rodriguez
Amy Anderson
Claudia Colberson
Danielle Donaldson
Evie Ezekial

Novice Class C 5'11" & over
Lilli Di Rossi
Shelli Smith
Fiona McFickleson
Tami Terrell
Folani Farell
Stephanie Story
Felicia Fitzpatrick

The expeditor will then usher the seven athletes in Novice Class A onto the stage. Only these seven Athletes will be on the stage for comparison rounds. Once comparisons rounds are complete, the judge will say, "Ladies, thank you and see you tonight." That is your clue that the judges are preparing to move on to Novice Class B, and then Novice Class C. The comparison rounds are complete. The judges have made their decisions.

Now let's skip to the awards ceremony at the night show. Each class will have a first, second, and third place winner. But in this situation, our focus is only on the first place winner because the first place winner is the only athlete that advances to get to the Overall.

The first place winner in each class is:

Novice Class A 5'0" – 5'4"
Mikaela Marcos

Novice Class B 5'5" – 5'9"
Amy Anderson

Novice Class C 5'11" & over
Lilli Di Rossi

Since these three athletes have won their class, they will remain on stage and go through comparison rounds together. The judges will now do live judging to determine who will be the 2021 Gladiator of All Muscle Women's Bikini Overall winner! Judges will still, regardless of height, judge all of the athletes together, using the same criterion: symmetry, muscle development, and conditioning. After live judging your top three winners are: Lilli Di Rossi (1), Mikaela Marcos (2), and Amy Anderson (3).

Lilli Di Rossi is your 2021 Gladiator of All Muscle Women's Bikini Overall winner!

In this specific example, Lilli Di Rossi will leave the show with at least one medal for winning her class and one medal for winning overall. Coming away from your show having won your class and overall is a big deal!

Now that you have a basic foundation, imagine arriving to the venue the morning of the show and finding the Order of Events taped on the wall. You see 50 names registered for Women's Bikini Novice Class A, 50 names registered in Women's Bikini Novice Class B, and 20 names registered for Novice Class C. That's 120 athletes total registered for Women's Bikini Novice. If you have registered for Women's Bikini Novice Class A, and you intend to win first place, you have 49 other athletes to beat to receive a medal at the end of the night.

This info is good for athletes who are considering entering shows in larger organizations. The NPC Battle of Texas is the largest show I have ever attended and worked. That show literally went for twenty-four hours. Every year, there are hundreds of athletes that register. That tells you something. That's a good show! Now you understand why bodybuilding is an all-day event. I have attended shows where it took two hours to judge Bikini alone. It is a popular category and is generally always at the end of the show. Why? Women's Bikini keeps bodies in seats. Men's Bodybuilding does too, but Women's Bikini is the moneymaker!

Consider allowing one of your first competitions to be in an organization that offers a natural division under its umbrella. The show is a bit smaller and you have the opportunity to find solid footing in the sport and decide with a clear head which direction you want to go.

Winning is winning, but winning overall is definitely the cherry on top!

Chapter 18

SASS AND CLASS

Perfect practice lends itself to confidence and confidence lends itself to having a little sass and class. You will need it while you are performing your mandatory poses during comparison rounds. I have seen many athletes try to sass and class it before even mastering the pivot. Do not skip steps. First, master the pivot into your quarter turn. Your feet should be twitching at all times. You should be able to pivot in your sleep. Once you have mastered your pivot, then add in your mandatory poses. In the bathroom, while you are on Zoom calls, any time you walk past a mirror, and when you see your reflection in the grocery store window. Anywhere and anytime is the perfect time and place to pivot.

Sass and class is a thing of beauty to be witnessed during comparison rounds. You will notice the athletes raise a hand. Raising a hand is an acknowledgement of two things. One you've heard the head judge call your number and two, it signals to the other athlete, *it's me that you're switching places with.* Look down the line, find the other athlete with her hand raised, and start switching places.

There are two important things to note here: first, once you have raised your hand to acknowledge your number being called, and just as you take the first step to switch places, always cross in front. Always walk in front of the line. Think about the main purpose for even being on stage in the first place. It is to be seen. To be seen by the judges, all of your fandom, the expeditors, and other competitors. Everyone! That is why you cross the line in front. It matters. It shows confidence. Also, as you are moving into place, strut. Strut confidently across the line of competitors, right in front of the judges' table, and take your time when you do it. Even when you are moving into place, you are being judged on how you move and how you reposition yourself. You definitely don't want to take all day, but certainly take a moment to strut your confidence right across the stage. That's sass and class.

> **Even when you are moving into place, you are being judged on how you move and how you reposition yourself.**

Second, you will see what I'm about to say often. So often, that it seems like the right thing to do. I am picking on the ladies here because most frequently, you will see this from female athletes. When an athlete's number is called and she raises her hand, nerves take over. She raises her hand and simultaneously half squats. The photographer inevitably takes your stage shot in the position that looks like you are using the toilet. When you hear your number called, think to yourself sass and class baby. Raise your hand high to acknowledge you have heard your number and then strut, don't squat; strut confidently across the front of the line, reposition yourself, and be ready to repeat the mandatory poses again. That's sass and class.

Chapter 19

SHOWS ARE WON FROM THE BACK

When I first started bodybuilding, I was so excited to get started. Up to that point, athletics had been one of the only constants in my life. I took a look at my training plans and my nutrition protocols. I was ready! I knew the gym and I have always been very comfortable in it. My coach handed me my training plan and said, "Take a look at this and let me know if there's anything you're not familiar with." I was confident that I would know everything!

I was in sheer disbelief! There were exercises on my training plan that I had never heard of before: Barbell Hip Thrusters and Barbell Glute Bridges. Single Arm Lat Pull Downs and Face Pulls. Cable Kickbacks, Donkey Calf Raises, and more! I'd heard of a regular calf raise, but never a Donkey Calf Raise! That is when my coach used a term I had never heard of before: mirror muscles.

I knew the gym, or so I thought, but I didn't know anything about attachments. So of course, that meant I knew nothing about the intentional use of an attachment. Stop for a second and think of all of the tools a sculptor may use to sculpt and mold his clay: a clay cutter, sponges, a small hammer, and at least seven different styles of chisels. Each of these tools change the appearance of the clay and produce a different result, yet each tool is critical to the appearance of the entire finished product. Attachments are the same, each attachment is a critical tool in designing the entire finished product: you!

Like so many people, many of my years in a gym were spent developing the muscles I could see. Although it seems ridiculously obvious, I knew there are muscles on the back side of my body in theory, but I assumed that by working the front, I was working the back as well. As I look back, I am chalking it up to *you don't know what you don't know*, and I didn't know.

> Like so many people, many of my years in a gym were spent developing the muscles I could see. Although it seems ridiculously obvious, I knew there were muscles on the back side of my body in theory, but I assumed that by working the front, I was working the back as well.

If you are one of the lucky few that have an actual bodybuilding gym in your area, you will know what I'm talking about and this next statement may not apply. For everyone else: really think about the last time you were in the gym and saw someone performing exercises that specifically targeted the muscles of the posterior chain. No, not that girl just standing in the mirror watching herself work her glutes, but the muscles of the entire backside, from the neck all the way down to the Achilles heel.

In bodybuilding, you will often hear the phrase, "Shows are won from the back." That means deliberately working the muscles you cannot see. Walk into the gym on a random Tuesday and you will find both men and women standing in the mirror grunting and working hard. Performing endless bicep curls, going "balls to the wall" on chest and "beast mode" on shoulders. Every now and then you will see someone sitting on the leg extension, and that is only to work the quads. What about the rest?

With every single body-building show I attended, I sat and I studied. When the muscles of the posterior side of the body are developed, the body looks like perfect sculpture frozen in time. When I look at the anterior side of the body, yes, of course, there are muscles. A bicep, a quad, maybe a great set of abs, sure.

But on the posterior chain, there are so many small and uniquely shaped muscles that can be identified by name. When you see those muscles on a lean physique, you are actually able to say to yourself, "That is the lower trap and those are rhomboids. Right there, there is her teres major. That is what the hamstring-glute connection looks like." The ability to sit in a seat and name each muscle clearly defined on a living human, as if you were studying an anatomy chart, is simply put, art. The judges know that the level of leanness a competitor must have to see that kind of muscle detail takes work!

Winning from the back is the ability to show muscle detail on your physique. Wide lats and a tiny taper in the waist, well developed glutes and the ability to see where the glutes end and the hamstrings begin, the ability to see where the muscles attach. Yes! You can see quads from viewing the body from the backside. Winning from the back is displaying a truly three-dimensional physique. Go to a show and see for yourself: are shows won from the back?

Chapter 20

PEAK WEEK

This is the week you and your coach have been waiting for! This week you will see the result of 16 weeks of committed effort: your body is about to peak. If you've been around bodybuilding, you've probably heard competitors say things like, "I peaked too soon," or "I looked better the next day." It happens. I distinctly remember checking into the host hotel on Friday night. I took my bags upstairs and caught a glimpse of myself in the mirror. I put my bags down and took a good look at myself: front, side, back, side. Because this was my first competition, I didn't really know what peaking too soon meant, but I knew my body. Intuitively, I knew I had peaked. I'll never forget it. It was Friday afternoon at 2:30 pm. That was the best I had ever looked. Ever.

During peak week, I was excited and losing my mind at the same time. My body fat was lower than it had ever been in my life! I remember several random moments of literally jumping up and down from excitement – think Will Ferrell in Elf – and then needing to immediately go sit down because, in my excitement, I had made myself lightheaded. During my peak week, I dropped another percent and a half of body fat. I stopped sleeping, and several times it felt like my body was just going to give out. Sheer excitement overshadowed all of this. The excitement of *I am really doing this* had set in.

During this week, you will want to be systematically executing details. Do exactly as you have been instructed. By now a phenomenal coach has given you a list of activities that need to be adjusted during peak week. Things like increasing your water intake for a few days and then dramatically decreasing water intake, no more leg day, light blood flow workouts, and a strategic plan for the sharp increase in carbohydrates as show day approaches. Expect your coach to request pictures and maybe even one final posing session. All is well. Just stay focused.

During peak week you will receive confirmations for the appointments you booked two months ago. I had almost forgotten until the emails started arriving in my inbox. I received an "everything you need to know" email from each service provider. Hair and makeup sent an updated time and room number. The tanning agency sent my time slot and official tanning location. In that same email was an attachment about how to bathe during peak week. No lotion and no deodorant! What? Now, if you are the fancy kind of girl and you go to a stylist for your hair, the lash bar for this, the wax center for that and Ms. Ling for the other, that's all good. However! Make sure you coordinate hair, make up, and lashes within 72 hours of the show. It stands to be repeated: make sure your hair appointment does not clash with your tan appointment. At a show where there are 100 athletes registered, you must be on time. It is better for you to be sitting there waiting for the professional than the other way around. You will miss your designated time slot trying to be high maintenance! Remember, be professional.

Be prepared to receive one final email about the athletes

meeting. The athletes meeting is a stab in the dark; you likely won't know what time it will be until you arrive at athlete check-in. Just know a meeting is coming. The meeting can either be at the host hotel or the venue the night before the show, or at the venue in the morning of the show.

One of the coolest things that happened to me during peak week was the fitting of my suit. On Monday, my suit still did not fit. By Thursday, it fit better. You or someone you know may have had a similar experience. This is the reason I continue to emphasize that you use the professionals whose craft is specific to competition. I totally get that you got a Bedazzler last year for Christmas and you have not used it yet, and have a fantastic swimsuit you bought two years ago for a special occasion, but trust me, competition day is not the special occasion. The professionals understand how the body is going to change in those final days.

Saturday morning my suit fit like a glove. It's peak week. It's on.

Chapter 21

PACK YOUR SHOW BAG
AND GET TO THE HOST HOTEL

Your show bag should be separate from the bag you pack to spend your nights at the host hotel. Your show bag is just that – it goes with you to the venue where your show is located – so either pack it separately or when you get to your hotel room, separate your items for the day ahead. I understand everyone's brain does not organize and compartmentalize information the same way. So, do what is best for you. But if I were you, I would pack my show bag completely separate, and pack it early.

I was like a little kid. I had my show bag packed eight weeks before show day. I simply designated a corner of my bedroom and laid my open suitcase on the floor. During my own prep, as I attended shows and observed, I created my own small list of items I wanted to have with me on show day. I would purchase the item and throw it in my show bag for later.

The day I received my suit in the mail, I was beyond excited! I opened the package, took a look at my suit, put the suit back in the mailing envelope, and tossed it in my Show Bag. If you

> I was like a little kid. I had my show bag packed eight weeks before show day.

are in any way the sort of person that gets frazzled, on show day the one thing that you would forget would be your suit, and inevitably, your first show will be two hours from home. At the end of the chapter, you will find a comprehensive list of items you'll want to pack in your show bag. Some items on the list you may not need, but pack them anyway, because another competitor will. There is no better way to build comradery backstage than to help another competitor super glue a runaway hair track or sew on a broken strap at the last minute!

The Host Hotel

The minute you have chosen your show, you will want to start looking for information about the host hotel. Read the fine print on the show's promotion material. The host hotel may be listed there, but if not, a simple Google search will do. Keep your eyes on your email, as the show promoter may offer a discount code. When you call, be sure to ask the receptionist, "Is this the host hotel for the Mr. Master of the Entire World bodybuilding competition?" Generally speaking, the show promoters have reserved, specific floors, blocks of rooms and a conference room or two for competitors and their families, hair and makeup, tanning, and in the natural divisions, a room for the polygraph test. So be sure you are in the right place!

Stay at the host hotel, because if your hair appointment is at 3:00 am, making two wrong turns and hitting a pothole in the rain, while simultaneously watching your GPS at 2:55 am is a recipe for disaster. It is much easier to wake up and walk down the hallway. Also, any last-minute announcements will make their way through the grapevine of the host hotel first; you definitely want to be in the know. Other competitors will be present; coaches, family members, fans, and sometimes the pros even show up. If you and your coach need to make any last minute posing adjustments or you feel you just need to run through some things again, the fitness center has mirrors.

Staying at the host hotel also allows you to step out and take care of your finishing touches before you have to wake up your support staff. Remember, show day is a long day for everyone and your fandom won't have the adrenaline rush that you will! The host hotel is where all of the action is. The energy is high and you will definitely want to experience that. Not to mention the complimentary breakfast for your fans who will be with you all day. The main point here is that as soon as you are able, reserve lodging at the Host Hotel.

> Tip: Do not let the maid service come in and clean! Inevitably an earring will fall into the blankets and you will send a family member back to look for it, but the bed has already been made. It's gone.

The polygraphy lasts about 30 minutes. If you have never taken a polygraph test, you're going to be nervous. Breathe, relax, and take your time before you respond. There's no penalty for nerves. "Yes," or "No." That is all.

Show Bag Checklist

- ☐ Competition Suit
- ☐ Posing heels
- ☐ Jewelry
- ☐ Needle and thread
- ☐ Super glue
- ☐ Vaseline
- ☐ Lip gloss
- ☐ Slippers, flip flops or slides
- ☐ Extra bikini bite
- ☐ Hair spray
- ☐ Curler or flat iron
- ☐ Makeup
- ☐ Tweezers
- ☐ Nail Clipper
- ☐ Extra set of eyelashes
- ☐ Resistance bands
- ☐ A set of dark sheets. Fitted and flat cover the sheets at the hotel.
- ☐ A fleece blanket or throw
- ☐ Pillow
- ☐ Music
- ☐ Headphones
- ☐ Charging cord with the wall plug
- ☐ Baby wipes
- ☐ Sanitary napkins
- ☐ Advil
- ☐ Sugary snack
- ☐ Food, don't forget your food!

See your Coach for any additional items he/she would like for you to add to the list.

- ☐ Additional items
- ☐ Additional items
- ☐ Additional items
- ☐ Additional items
- ☐ Additional items

Chapter 22

ATHLETE CHECK-IN

Athlete check-in is the evening before the show. The most interesting observation I've had about athlete check-in is the energy. The energy is both high and low at the same time. Energy is high because the athletes are truly excited – the day they've been prepping for, for months has finally arrived! It is also low because athletes are truly exhausted and depleted. You can actually feel the I-want-to-be-excited-but-I'm-too-tired vibe. After four months of preparation, it's all starting to come together, and you can feel it.

Athlete check-in is just as it sounds: there will be someone sitting at a table matching your name, and double checking the categories you've signed up for. For example: "Natasha Jones, right. Perfect. Looks like you've signed up for Women's Figure Novice and Women's Figure Master. Excellent, you're good to go."

Next, you will receive your number and you will be instructed on which side to wear your number. At one of the last shows I worked; pros were instructed to wear their numbers on the opposite side of the Amateurs. Be aware of this, just because you have been instructed to do one thing and you see some-one else doing something differently, does not mean either of you are wrong. They may have been given pro instructions and there is no way of knowing who's who until the Pro divisions are called and you actually see them on stage, unless of course you know them personally, or follow them on Instagram.

Unless you have competed in the organization before, ath-lete check-in is the first time you become a face to the judges, and not just a registration number. This is also the first time you will see the other competitors and the "sizing up" begins. I remember my first competition. Somewhere around three weeks out, it hit me that I had no idea who was going to show up that day. I had no idea how many other athletes had regis-tered for my division; you won't find out until the morning of the show. The not knowing was intimidating, but it definitely made me work harder.

What you can expect

Everyone will be in good spirits, but tired. You will meet the show promoters. They will be scurrying around putting the final touches on every detail of the show. It has always been easiest for me to identify the show promoters because they are almost always wearing a shirt with the name of their show on it – Shredded Muscle Mania, Max Muscle Mayhem, Long Horn Lollapalooza, you catch my drift. The other competitors will be in loose athletic clothing or a robe from either having just fin-ished tanning or about to go to their appointment.

The biggest takeaway from this chapter is this: You don't know who's who in the room. Walk into the room and be on your best behavior. What I mean by *who's who* is *everybody* is in that room: The show promoters, the judges, other competitors, coaches, people who don't look like they're competing, etc. Be careful what you say and who you say it to because you don't know who you are talking to. Be warm, inviting, and even appreciative for the opportunity to compete on the stage with other greats.

> Be careful what you say and who you say it to because you don't know who you are talking to.

Here are a few items that fall under athlete check-in:

1. Matching athletes name with face and registration numbers.
2. Receive competition number to be pinned to suit or trunks.
3. Updated tanning appointment
4. Receive updated hair and makeup times - It is not uncommon to receive an email that basically says "Show up to a random room number at some ungodly hour."
5. Height check - Let's say you have so many competitors there is no way everyone can be on the stage at the same time. A division will then be broken into height classes.
6. Organization card - If you have not purchased your organization card, you will be required to do so before you get on stage.
7. Swag bag - Your T-shirt and other goodies that thank you for being an athlete in this organization.
8. Purchase your stage shots - I completely missed the memo about stage shots. Buy them! These are professional photos of you and only you on stage. You won't be sorry.

Chapter 23

ICING ON THE CAKE

Think of tanning, gluing, and glazing as icing on the cake. One of the first things you may notice about the sport of bodybuilding is the tan.

Tanning, gluing, and glazing is, to me, the most fascinating aspect of the sport. It is also my favorite. Sixteen weeks of incredibly disciplined hard work come down to a perfectly laid tan, a perfectly glued suit, and loving hands to glaze your body.

Why do bodybuilders tan? Well, there are several reasons. All of it is an illusion and that's the coolest part. The tan is a part of the illusion. Let's be clear, nothing about the tan is supposed to look natural, so don't freak out. The purpose of your tan is to enhance your hard work. Your tan adds depth, contour, and precision to your muscles. It enhances your conditioning and smooths out skin blemishes, such as birth marks, discolorations, and—depending on the tanning products and buffing creams—even tattoos.

In most venues, the stage lights are mounted directly over the stage, meaning directly over you, the athlete. Additionally, there may be a light pointed directly at the stage mounted out over the audience. Generally, you will find some pretty harsh overhead white light at all venues. The lighting, of course, is bright and designed for you, as an athlete to be seen. The down side to this harsh white light is, it literally washes the color off of you.

Without any treatment to your skin, everybody looks either white, ashy, or pale. Don't forget, you've entered this show to be compared to other people; so, without a tan you will practically be unseen. Your fans are sitting in the audience to see your hard work, let them see it. Because humans are a mix of chemicals, some folks will turn green in places like underarms, and around the pubic hair line. I've even seen the greenish color at the back of the knees. The reason for this greenish color is your natural hormones and body chemistry responding to the chemicals in the tan. In general, you may see this greenish color appear where you perspire most.

During your comparison rounds, it will be blatantly obvious that you did not tan or glaze. Your skin will look dull and ashy. I have seen it many, many times. And I have to put it out there, it is people of color who think they don't need to tan or their coach didn't feel comfortable telling them to tan. They feel they are dark enough, and in most cases they are, but a competitive bodybuilding show is not most cases. No one, and I mean no one, is ever naturally dark enough under harsh white stage lights.

I've seen it with my own eyes. Offstage I saw an African American female walking around the auditorium. She was a very nice shade of dark chocolate. Her skin was smooth, much like a Nestle chocolate bar had been melted all over her skin. I didn't know anything about her, I just remember seeing her. Once she got on stage, I didn't even recognize her as the same person. The overhead stage lights washed the color right off. She looked beige at best. Think about it, If she didn't tan, that probably means she didn't do much glazing either and we'll get to that in a moment. So, in addition to being beige at best, she looked dry. Let it be said here and now, people of color need a spray tan.

Remember, these are comparison rounds, you will stand out, but not in a good way.

On show day, I had three coats of tan. One from the night before, one in the morning before prejudging, and a touch up just before the night show began. Three coats. Why would you leave a sixteen-week prep to chance at the very end, at the final hour? Don't!

Let's get down to the nitty gritty. In this chapter you'll find useful tips on tanning, gluing, and glazing.

Tanning

In your peak week emails, you will receive a time slot from the tanning agency. Please be on time. Depending on the size of the show, the email will also request that you show up with your division. The email will read something like

Tanning Appointment: Women's Figure
7:00 pm – 8:00 pm.

You may show up anytime in that one-hour window. But let's clear something up right now, there are people out there who believe they are too important to wait. They are impatient and have in their minds, *I don't want to sit and wait so I'm going to show up right at 7:59 pm.* It doesn't matter when you arrive, be prepared to wait. You are waiting because, while the tanners know how many people preregistered for tans, there is no way to predict how many of them will show up late—traffic, missed plane, hair and makeup ran over—so expect to wait. A body-building show is a day of waiting. The professional tanners are moving athletes through like cattle in a shoot. Again, depending on the size of the show, more than 250 bodies can be tanned in one evening. Be professional and wait patiently.

Your first coat of tan will be applied the night before the show. You will be called to one of two locations, either one of the conference rooms inside of the host hotel or the venue where the actual show will take place. Expect to tan naked. Everyone. Guys, you will be given a sock. Stuff your fruit and berries in the sock, stand patiently in a dry tent and wait to be called into a spray tent. As a professional, it is very awkward for me, to have to explain to you how to stuff your fruit and berries into a sock, especially since I don't have any. Even if you don't yet possess a Pro card, it is a good to practice behaving like one. Handle everything professionally, no matter how awkward.

When you arrive for your appointment, expect to see a row of pop-up tents propped side by side. Depending on the number of athletes registered there will be two to four spray tents, and the others are designated as drying tents. You will be shuffled into a tent. There are two sides. Most organizations now require that men and women tan separately on two separate sides. There was a time not so long ago where women and men would be standing in tents next to one another. Even if you are in close proximity, there should be a men's side and a women's side. Both men and women may enter the same conference room door, but after that, women will go left and men will go right.

It's super important to listen to where the tanner asks you to put your clothes. If you didn't hear ask, "Where would you like me to put my clothes." In most cases, you will be instructed to place your clothes inside the tent in the front corner. I strongly recommend folding each article of clothing neatly and then stacking them on the ground. I also recommend arriving with no jewelry—that includes wedding rings, toe rings and other pieces of jewelry, even if you've vowed never to remove them.

A: the tanner will request that you remove it. If you chose not to, that's fine, but please know that by the time you are asked to remove that item, you will be naked and there won't be a family member nearby to hand your item to. As to not be held responsible, the tanner likely won't hold it for you. So where does your jewelry go? You toss your jewelry in the same place where you tossed your clothes. Inevitably, you'll forget you took it off, pick up your shirt to put it on and your jewelry goes flying across the room somewhere. You won't realize it until you are back in your home city. If you're lucky, the tanners will find your jewelry when they break down.

B: You keep the ring on and the tanner tans over it.

The tan takes about 15 minutes to dry. Prepare yourself, the spray is cold! To keep the spray contained and to aid in the tans setting faster on your skin, there will be industrial sized fans placed between the tents. It's cold back there!

I strongly recommend using the official tanner of the show. All shows have an official tanner. Look at your show promotion material and you will see a logo or some affiliated tanning information. Tanning will typically be done at the host hotel or at the venue where the bodybuilding show will be held. Keep up with your emails. It is no fun driving around, most likely at night, with a car full of family, carb-depleted, hungry, in an unfamiliar city looking for your tanner.

So that you are able behave like a professional, here are a

few tips:

1. Know your body. You look at yourself in the mirror every day. You know what blemishes you have and which stretch marks you wish weren't there. You know which arm is darker than the other and how your feet never quite "even out" in the summer. Apply your knowledge; have those blemishes and marks evened out with a professional spray tan.

2. Listen, watch, and remember. Listen to which side of the room the tanner directs you to. Listen to where the tanner asks you to place your clothes. Watch the flow of traffic. Remember which athletes entered before and after you – there is a certain point where all the naked bodies look the same. I promise the tanners are not skipping you, all you'll have on is a hairnet and since you are naked, we have nothing to identify you by – just give a shout and say "I'm next!"

3. Don't be high maintenance. If this is your first show, acting high maintenance is the first indicator that you've never done this before. Remember the Women's Pro Figure at the Dallas Europa example? The real pros know the tan is the icing on the cake, and they stand there quietly. They don't watch, they look straight ahead. They allow the professionals to work. In short, be classy. Smile, say thank you. Ask the tanners "How's your day so far?" Turn around and get your tan.

4. Bring a hair net and hair clip just in case. The tanning agency typically provides plenty of these items. But inevitably overnight, 25 last-minute registrations come

through. The tanning agency has already packed their cases and are likely already setting up on-location when those extra numbers come through. Bring your own items. Again, just be prepared and you won't have to sweat it.

5. Guys, please bring your own sock. Do not – I repeat – do not hand the tanner your sock when you are done receiving your tanning service. You may however ask, "Where would you like me to put this?" or bring your own sock, remove it, get dressed, put it in your pocket and walk out with your head held high just like the pros do.

6. Urine. Let's talk about it. Now this piece of advice goes for both guys and girls. There's really no other way around it: once you're glued in you cannot go to the restroom. I'll talk a little bit more about this in the gluing section. Urine stains your tan. If you find yourself in a situation where you absolutely must go to the restroom and you accidently pee on yourself or have urine running down your leg, know this:

   A. That is a novice mistake and you will get major side eyes from girls who've done it before.

   B. Laugh it off, no worries, your tanning team are professionals, they've got a product just for you. They'll use a bit of product and a buffing mitt and blend those stains right out.

7. Be respectful: cover everything. Once your body is tanned, you are sticky and wherever you go and whatever

you touch, you will leave sticky tan behind. If you've followed the "Week of" tanning instructions, you'll know that you already stink. Now you're stinky and leaving tan everywhere you go. Cover everything! Car seats, hotel bed, toilet seat and anything else you may rub on or brush against for the next several days.

8. Follow the "week of" tanning instructions. Your tan will lay better on your skin if you've exfoliated as instructed in your email. Also, if you're a bikini athlete, part of judging criteria is skin tone. Again, this is a business. This is a part of knowing your profession, and your craft. If you want to be a professional, start here: follow the instructions to the letter and bring dark and loose clothing to change into after your tan. Just so you know, some tanning agencies ask that you do not use deodorant a few days prior to receiving services. Be prepared for that. Deodorant and tanning solution don't mix.

> You need a professional. And not just any professional, but a professional that knows stage makeup. One who knows lighting and how makeup and skin tone are affected by lighting.

Gluing

Ultimately, it is your choice to have your bikini top and bottom glued.

So that you are able to behave like a professional, here's some advice on gluing:

1. The person gluing you will likely be seated. As you approach the front of the line, start pay attention and listening to the questions being asked of the other athletes. Approach the chair and be prepared for them to ask, "Do you want your bra cups glued also?" At this time, it is your responsibility, to think back to the last few weeks of prep when your posing coach told you it was time to start practicing in your suit. When you hit your side pose, did you feel a little nervous or paranoid that things may move or fall out? If so, the answer is "Yes, please, I want my top glued."

2. Hit your back pose. When you have your bikini bottom glued, turn around and hit your back pose. Tip your hips and arch your back. Your back pose is the most important in gluing. Your tanning professional is literally gluing your suit in place so that when you hit your back pose, the suit doesn't ride up and turn into a thong. The entire bottom will be glued in place.

3. Wax everything. I am not necessarily saying you need a Brazilian, but please wax everything that may be exposed. The test? Turn around and hit your back pose.

Glazing

Tanning and glazing go together. Now is the appropriate time to get greased up and shiny like your first day of kindergarten. Think of your tan and glaze as icing on the cake. A birthday cake is nice, but what is it without the white icing, lavender flowers, and your name written in pink piping? It's nothing. Glaze is a part of your presentation. Otherwise, your skin will appear dull. Glaze can be one of many things. Vaseline, wig spray, grapeseed oil, or a specialty concoction created by your tanner.

So that you are able to behave like a professional, here's a bit of advice on glazing:

1. Know your skin-type. Especially guys. If you have dry skin, kindly ask for a little extra glaze because by the time you are glazed, stand in line and wait to be called to the stage, your skin will have sucked that little bit of glaze up, and your skin will yet again, have a dull appearance.

Show Day is your party!

2. Balance. You don't want to look slippery, but when the light hits you, you want to glow.

3. Trust the professionals' eye. As product is being applied, your tanner is simultaneously watching your skin suck in and devour the product. So, while you may walk away feeling and looking a bit slippery, by the time you stand in line and finally get to the stage fifteen minutes later, you'll be perfect. I still think that knowing your skin type is the best piece of advice. Then and only then will you know how much glaze you want.

Chapter 24

SHOW DAY:
ORDER OF EVENTS, BACKSTAGE, PUMPING UP AND YOUR SUGARY SNACK

The energy at a bodybuilding show can truly make you feel bipolar. It's gritting your teeth, holding the side of a chair until you're white-knuckled, it's having a bundle of nerves, there's screaming and yelling from your fans and then all at once, you've got to pull yourself together, walk across the stage, turn it on and perform. I have been studying bodybuilding shows for 15 years. Every show is pretty high-energy and the music is amazing. Show day is your party!

At your party, anything that could possibly go wrong will. The show will not start on time. Your suit will lose a stone, your heel will break, a hairpiece will fall out, you will pee on your leg. Guys, your posing trunks will split up the rear seam or even worse the front. You will forget your posing trunks. You will leave your food at the hotel and maid service has already come.

The order of events will change and you've already pumped up and eaten your last marshmallow. Your posing music will not play on the system at the venue. I once entered and exited the stage four times. Four. And finally, on the fifth try, my music decided to play.

In the morning during prejudging, all Divisions will walk and pose to whichever music the house DJ selects. If the DJ plays Tupac, walk. If the DJ plays the Guns N Roses, walk. At every show I've attended, the DJ was really good about keeping the energy exactly where it is supposed to be! At the evening show, Men's Bodybuilding, Women's Bodybuilding, Men's Classic Physique and Women's Physique will perform a posing routine; Amateurs have sixty seconds to perform, Pros have ninety seconds. Before Prep (like now) start listening to music differently. Find a song you like, a song you feel confident posing to and a song that communicates your personality to the audience and judges. About two weeks before the show, be prepared to receive an email requesting that you submit your music. Make sure your music is precut and edited down to your allotted time. Submit your music file in the exact format that is requested of you or your music won't play. Trust me, I know.

Show day is still a party! Shake it off and stay focused. You were born for this!

In the past 72 hours you should have been receiving some pretty explicit instructions from your coach. One of those instructions should have been to be sure you attend the athlete's meeting. At the athlete's meeting the show promoters will discuss what's called the order of events. The order of events will likely be scheduled a few months in advance. But you can guarantee on the day of the show the order of events will change. Usually, men's and women's bodybuilding are first. The order of events should be printed on a piece of white paper and posted visibly backstage for the expeditors, athletes, and coaches to see. When you first arrive at the venue, the order of events, may not actually be printed and ready to go yet. Perhaps show promoters are still finalizing numbers and putting finishing touches on the event. However, by the time the show starts, look around for pieces of white paper taped to the wall. That is your order of events. Find it, take a picture of it and send it to your coach. A phenomenal coach will tell their athlete to take a picture of the order of events and send it to them. The reason your coach should be asking you for the order of events is that it determines when you will begin pumping up. Pumping up too soon or not having enough time to pump matters! That is why sending the order of events to your Coach is extremely important.

Most of the time Men's Bodybuilding is first, followed by Men's Classic Bodybuilding, Women's Bodybuilding, Women's Physique, and from there, you will find several other possible variations. Most of the time you can expect to see this order or some version of it.

Backstage, Pumping Up, & Your Sugary Snack

When you see backstage footage of bodybuilding shows, you will most always see athletes doing what's called pumping up. Pumping up literally refers to pumping up the muscles with a nice flush of blood in the moments before stepping onto the stage. Flushing the muscles with blood gives muscles a nice full, swollen, and plump appearance.

The tool that each athlete uses to achieve the pump is different, and you will see those differences backstage. Some athletes' muscles pump up perfectly well using only resistance bands, while others prefer to use lightweight dumbbells. You may also see some athletes running through a full workout. I have actually been backstage at some shows that provide athletes with a full set of weights and a pull-up/dip stand power tower. The pump up area looked like a mini gym. Watching the athletes respond to having that much equipment available to them was pretty awesome. Both male and female athletes were like kids in a candy store.

There is a bit of bodybuilding lore around pumping up the lower half. On several occasions, I have heard through the coach and competitor grapevine, that pumping the legs prior to stepping on stage is a no-no. The legs hold so much blood, the pump makes the legs appear swollen and bloated, not lean. Some people believe pumping up the legs has the opposite effect on the legs than it does the rest of the body. I remember seeing a female competitor backstage doing DB Squats. Her legs popped! The legs were super lean and tight. You and your coach will decide.

As for me, I used resistance bands. I used resistance bands because that is what I saw everyone else doing. Hindsight, I should have used heavier weights. I know my body and my muscles are not at all amused by resistance bands, and no, I'm not here to argue the effectiveness of a total body resistance band workout. That's a different subject altogether. The fact of the matter is, I needed a 20-pound dumbbell to get my party started!

That is why I will continue to say, you know your body best. On the days at the gym when you look at yourself in the mirror and say, "Well look at me," remember that. The exercise you just performed is the exercise you want to file away for your pump up. There will be times during your backstage pump when you know a muscle is there. You are saying to yourself, "I can't see my obliques and I know they are there," do what you know. Perform the exercises that you know will bring your muscles to the edges of your skin.

If the show promoter allows a member of your crew to purchase a backstage pass, do it. They will very much enjoy helping you with the very last part of the process. Pumping up and feeding you your sugary snack. Especially, if you have had a difficult prep and have not been the nicest, it is awesome to let them in on this part of your process. I did. In the moments before I stepped on stage, I felt like a mini celebrity pumping up and having my, yet again phenomenal coach feed me a Pop-Tart® while I was pumping up.

"Always have someone there to help you remember, like a responsible assistant. Prepare a checklist of things you need and give it to them the night before. You can never have too much. Prepare a couple extra meals. Have a couple of suits. Pack as much as you can with someone the night before while going over the checklist. Some venues are bare bones when it comes to resources. This minimizes stress during show day. If you have someone with you if something did get missed they can go get it."

—Matt Storm, GBO Pro Men's Beach Body Athlete, GBO Certified Judge, GBO Arizona/California State Director, Storm Classic/Global Open/Global Invitational Promoter

However, the next time I compete I will not use a Pop-Tart®, I will use a biscuit of some sort. These are the little nuance you learn. I learned later, months later, that actually a plain biscuit from McDonalds would have been best for me during pump up. Find yours. I remember talking to a guy backstage in Dallas, and he had created his own sweet potato soufflé with mini marshmallows in it and he looked amazing. I will continue to go back and stand on the fact that you are in your body 24/7, and you know best how your body responds to anything you put in it. Take note and communicate that information to your coach and go with it!

Until it's time for you to pump up, sit down. When you are backstage, you will see athletes laid out with a pillow and blanket, feet up on a chair or on a wall with their headphones in, take note. It's tempting to get caught up in the foray. You will surely see other competitors clamoring, tiptoeing, walking around the venue, in the audience, then backstage, just running around to be seen. I call it wasting energy and raising your cortisol levels. Go sit down. If it were me, I'd lay down and stay covered up and until the expeditor calls for my category. Keep your feet up on the wall and lay down. Think back to the Women's Pro Figure Pros. What would they do?

The bottom line: pumping up and your sugary snack are essentials. The two combined are magic and create the lean, tight, and hard stage ready, competitive appearance.

It's show day, it's your party, and this is really about to happen!

Be careful in the pump up area As the day turns into evening, the entire backstage area becomes like an ice rink. Divisions that don't wear shoes are closer to the beginning of the show and are glazed first. Athletes walk off the tarp and glaze tracks itself onto the venue floor as well. Be careful. If you are wearing heels, please, please be careful! This is another reason to stay off of your feet, keep still and sit down.

Chapter 25

ON ADDICTION & THE LOOK

My coach told me from the very beginning, "It's difficult to maintain the look. If you're considering competition again, we can't wreck your metabolism, you have to reverse out of the process the same way we went in." And boy was she right. Any good coach should be telling you that. Stage levels of leanness are not healthy to maintain.

A few weeks out from show day, I started to take an herbal diuretic.

The purpose the diuretic is to get rid of the last little bits of water your body is holding onto for dear life. For me, my over-the-counter diuretic took about one hour to hit my system. What I mean by *hit my system* is, I could visually see and feel the effects of the diuretic. I could see the effects as in, my body started to look dry. I could feel it. Since the purpose of the herbal diuretic is to release water, I was thirsty, my tongue was sticking to the roof of my mouth, and my nose was dry. In bodybuilding you will hear the phrases *looking dry* or *needing to dry out*. Those phrases don't only mean your mouth and nose dry out, it means your body is actually dropping water and becoming more defined. In two hours, it looked like I'd lost 2-3 pounds through my mid-section, especially in the hips. I looked good, but I felt awful! And even though I felt awful, I distinctly remember asking my coach twice backstage if I could take another diuretic.

> I looked good, but I felt awful!
> And even though I felt awful,
> I distinctly remember asking
> my coach twice backstage if I
> could take another diuretic.

In just 48 hours I had gotten addicted to the look and what that pill was doing to my body. I could see it and feel it. Addiction comes in many forms. For us, it's addicted to the look. The leanness of the look. The look of seeing the muscle you have worked so hard for finally appearing. I saw it and wanted it to stay forever! Despite the grueling work and countless hours of fasted cardio, and only one cup of spinach, I was not at all phased by the work once I saw the look take shape.

Chapter 26

POST PREP BLUES
& REVERSING OUT

In the days after show day, commonly referred to as post prep, I guarantee you will have several startling realizations. I had heard the competitors before me talk about post prep blues; you will probably hear about them too. I would hear competitors huddled together saying things like, "Yeah I had post prep blues too. It's bad." and "I just didn't know what to do with myself next." Nobody ever told me exactly what post prep blues were, so I just sat back and kind of waited around for them to show up.

Your fans and family members clamor around you with such awe and amazement, saying things like "I'm sure you can't wait to eat. What do you want your post show meal to be?" Post show meal this, pizza and pancakes that. In all the post show pictures I had ever seen; I saw competitors shoving donuts in their face and smiling. I thought to myself *okay, that must be what was expected of me*. I know I am preaching to the choir here, but after eating 25 grams of carbs for eight weeks and having my water cut to down to sips on show day, I wanted to sit down.

I was frustrated because joy, peace, laughter, and food were expected from me by the people around me.*

About an hour after having my glass plaques handed to me, my version of post prep blues hit. Medals in hand, I slid into the passenger seat of the car, laid my head back on the seat, and said, "I'm exhausted. All I want is a cup of water." The instant I sat down, it felt like a ton of bricks had collapsed in my lap. I remember the feeling like it was yesterday. I went back to my room in the host hotel, drank a cup of water and took a hot shower. I stood in the shower and watched the clear water running over my toes turn a shade of muddy brown. My feet disappeared as the tan washed off my body; the water was taking other things with it.

In the past 364 days, I had started a 16-week Prep when my mom passed away. I went home and buried my mother. I reentered prep, then had a car accident which resulted in a severe concussion eight weeks out from my next planned show. I laid on ice daily for 14 days and did nothing but think about winning. Come to find out, those fourteen days were the beginning of the healing process. Forty-five minutes of fasted cardio, seven days a week. Six days a week lifting with ten minutes post workout cardio. Twenty minutes of cardio before bed. Seven days a week, in between a full schedule of clients, in between life, in between grief. It had to get done. Period.

Prep took everything out of me. I mean everything. Whatever I did have left in me, I left it on the stage. I told my coach several times, "I don't have another Prep in me." Our plan was to do another show two weeks later. I was already in super shape and could have very easily dropped one or two more percentages

---

* I found it interesting that even after a bodybuilding competition, the event is celebrated with food!

in body fat, but I told my Coach, "I can't give anything else to this anymore."

I distinctly remember wanting to do nothing. All I wanted to do was lay in the bed in a quiet room, in the dark, and stare at the TV on mute. The only energy I had left was to move my eyeballs, just barely at that.

Post show I was sad for twelve months; the adrenaline that had kept me going had immediately worn off. My adrenals were tired; they asked me, *are you done yet, because we are*! I was exhausted. I could hardly form a complete sentence. I thought post-leg day was bad. All I could do was lay and think. Physically, I was done, I literally had no words. I could not form them. I just needed to lay and reflect. It was over. I needed some major quiet.

Competitors don't much discuss the mental aspects of the sport; you really don't hear about that. Everything is beast mode, grind harder, clap for yourself, the party, the endorsements, the newest supplement, the latest leggings, who's better than who, the best workout for your glutes. It's all so shiny. I know I am not alone when I say my body fat was low, and I felt like I was losing my mind.

On Reversing Out

Every coach is different and I say that because really only you and your coach know exactly what you had to do to get to the stage. Once I was ready to eat, I called my coach and told her I was ready. She said, "Your first meal should be what you want." I got dressed and drove to my favorite Mexican restaurant. I ordered a three flautas dinner and I was quite satisfied. I had not eaten there in eighteen months. Trust me on this, refried beans had never tasted so good!

After that, we began our reversing out. Again, every coach's approach to reversing out is different. I know your neighbor's cousin is going to tell you what she did, and the girl at the gym with the cool leggings is going to tell you what her boyfriend's ex did. Believe me, I know. But so that you don't gain thirty pounds in three weeks, reversing out is your coach's decision.

I learned very quickly that what got me to the stage – the character traits – and the motivations that got me through two winters of heavy lifting, and even the desire to go through a prep, was not going to be the same stuff that gets me to or even through the next phase. I found profound philosophical knowledge in that alone. What got me here wasn't going to be the same I needed to get me there, wherever there is.

My post prep blues set in when I realized this part of the journey was over and it made me sad.

Chapter 27

PICK THE RIGHT COACH FROM THE BEGINNING

What you want to see when you look in the mirror is the only thing that defines results; that is all that matters. I personally enjoy looking a little beefy and a little like I could kick down a door, but the next woman, may not want that look. Therefore, how each of us defines results is different.

Most every coach I know, wants their clients to feel better, move better, live better, and arrive happily at their results, with their mental health intact. The client/coach dynamic is a unique and special partnership, and in that partnership, there should be elements of a successful relationship: honesty, trust, compassion, integrity, loyalty, respect, and someone to tell you, "No!"

> You are picking someone who will be in your life for at least nine months to one year. You are paying someone to tell you when to eat, what to eat, how much to eat, and how long to work. There must be a measure of compatibility and respect for their authority.

The Initial Consult

During the initial consult, you are going to be excited. After all, you are talking to the individual that is going to help you achieve your goals! I am quite certain you will be thinking about outcome and results-related questions, as you should be. But there are several other aspects of the client/coach dynamic that seem obvious, yet are easy to overlook. Communication style, accessibility, boundaries, expectations, clear and realistic goals, and the manner in which your exercise programming will be delivered, are just a few additional considerations. Along with a coach sending you out the door with a quality program to execute, the items above hold equal value and can quickly overshadow and color your experience, either positively or negatively.

On your initial consult, listen carefully to your potential coach's responses and read between the lines. Just because you are sitting across the table from an industry expert, does not mean this person will be *your* industry expert. Follow your intuition without wavering. If a single part of the intake process is off, I can guarantee something else will be off. No, I'm not talking about the coach simply rushing in five minutes late, due to the five-car pileup that you were sitting behind too. No, not that. I'm talking about feelings and vibes we humans pick up on, but too often ignore because we want something.

The individual, the individual's coaching style, a*nd* the individual's communication style can make or break your experience. I have learned that communication is the most important. Believe it or not, something as simple as the client onboarding procedure, falls under communication.

While you're searching for the right coach, if you find that you, and the coach you are initiating contact with are missing each other, let that be information to you. From the time you make the initial contact with your potential coach, to the time you receive your workout program and nutrition protocol in hand, should be about one week. That is reasonable. It doesn't matter how amazing a coach's before and after pictures are, if there is lousy communication during the initial engagements.

During my time sitting across from potential clients in consults, I found there were many more questions that should have been asked, but weren't. A phenomenal coach will be more than forthcoming, and never vague.

Below you will find several general topics that you will want to ask directly. Ask as many of these questions as you possibly can, and any other questions that you can think of.

Is this your primary business, or do you work another job?

However you choose to word the question, you are asking, "How much time do you have for me and how responsive will you be to me?" You are asking your coach to set and manage expectations around time.

What time of day do you typically communicate with your clients?

Many fitness professionals are entrepreneurs; if I'm awake, I'm working. But boundaries around communication times are still important. Saturday night during date night probably is not the ideal time to respond to a client just because *she* is at the grocery store and has a question. From a coaching perspective, I understand the client who works the 48-hour firefighter shift, and texts me questions on the slow overnights at the fire house. I expect *him* to text me at strange hours, but the expectation of me as your coach would be that I respond to you the next day during my office hours.

On the flip side, what if your coach does have another job and works third shift, and you two are constantly missing each other? Without an explanation during the initial consult, in a very short while missing communication will become frustrating, and you will deem your new coach unresponsive.

During the initial consult, a simple, *"I'm a night owl, I do some of my best thinking and planning in the wee hours of the morning and because of that, I may text you. Please don't feel obligated to respond, just know that I was up working, respond to me when you're available."* This short statement works for both the client and the coach. It establishes some boundaries around the dynamic.

> **My degree is in History so I completely understand the concept of globalization, one of the positive impacts of globalization is the economy never sleeps. Still, put boundaries around communication times!**

How long should I expect the delay in communication to be?

The short answer twenty four hours. This is a dynamic relationship *and* it is business. If your doctor's office doesn't call you back within twenty four hours, like any human, your brain starts working and typically not for the better. *The doctor's office hasn't called back, maybe they lost my records, maybe it's something bad and they need to refer me to other doctors.* Sure, there is a saying that "No news is no news," but we are humans. We want to know.

When your Coach tells you "Give me a bit and I'll pull your nutrition plan together," but seven days later you still have not heard from him, you shoot a brief and polite text that says ,"Hey let me know what's next!" and you still hear nothing; anyone who's been in prep knows, that four days makes a difference, especially if you need to go to the grocery store based on adjustments to your nutrition plan. I understand that life happens; your coach is a person and is juggling lots, so have patience, yes. But I tend to lean towards *lack of time management* and *this is business.*

How often do you communicate with your clients?

This depends on your goals and how closely your coach wants to monitor your progress. I think every other week is reasonable. Some clients prefer once a month, at the beginning of the month, to set them straight. It depends, but definitely ask.

How often do you expect me to communicate with you?

In my experience, clients seems to be at polar opposite ends of the spectrum. On one end of the spectrum, there are clients that text you every day with a new realization about their body or a super specific question about a macro. On the other end of the spectrum, there are clients who pop up once a month with one question and they are truly happy out there, executing their plans independently. Everyone else fits somewhere in between.

How do you define clear and realistic goals?

This is something your coach should be asking you and you should be asking your coach. There was a time in my life when training on a six-day split, ninety minutes a day, eating thirty prepped meals and one cheater meal at Chick-fil-A on Saturday, was clear and realistic. There have been times where clear and realistic is a thirty-minute full body circuit. At other times in my life, clear and realistic was a twenty-minute low intensity walk in the middle of the day. Clear and realistic is not always "beast mode" and "going hard." Clear and realistic lends itself to consistency. How *you* remain consistent is a moving target. As an athlete, keep account of where you are mentally at all times and communicate that with your coach. That will help *both* of you continue to define clear and realistic.

What is your training style?

Most coaches have a philosophical foundation from which they work. If you hire a coach that is a former bodybuilder and you walk into the office and say "I don't eat carbs," that consultation may not go well. *Expect* to lift weights and *expect* to eat a healthy amount of carbohydrates. If you hire a former cyclist to be your coach, expect some foundation in cycling as a part of your cardio training program. If you are looking for a High-intensity interval training (HIIT) program, I am not your person. Yes, as a client, you may want the coach to deliver something; but all coaches have a style, and quite frankly they don't have to change that style for you. Their style makes them phenomenal at what they do. Respect the coach enough, to allow him or her to stay in their lane of mastery. Do *your* due diligence and make sure you find a coach whose training style aligns with what you are looking for, and what you need.

> Yes, you absolutely want a coach that is up-to-date on industry standards! But you do not want a coach that is trying to show you all the new stuff, especially if the new stuff has nothing to do with **you** liking what **you** see when **you** look in the mirror—your definition of results!

Which virtual platform do you use?

Some platforms are not as user-friendly. That makes a difference at 7:00 am, after standing for a twelve-hour nursing shift and you have mustered what is left of your energy to get to the gym. Now you are standing on the gym floor fighting with your virtual platform. That it not quite the recipe for success you had imagined.

For me, I'm an analog girl and this is a digital world. I still prefer to walk into the gym with my workout printed on paper, folded on a small clipboard, and a mechanical pencil. It never fails, when my phone is in my hand, I somehow end up checking emails. Knowing that about yourself is information you need to take with you to your consult. Picking the right coach is as much about the person, as it is *how* they deliver their product. It seems like a small thing, but make sure you are comfortable using a digital platform.

How many days a week are your training plans?

You want a coach that is going to listen to your needs. A weight loss program will have different training requirements than an athlete sculpting a physique for a bodybuilding competition. Remember that honesty piece? You have to be honest with yourself, and your Coach about what you are *really* willing to execute. In your head, you may be in the gym six days a week. But in real life, three days a week is clear, realistic, and what is actually happening. Communicate where you *really* are with your potential Coach.

How much do you trust your client's knowledge of his or her own body?

I'm not talking about a client who says, "I like eating potato chips because they make me feel good." No! You have been in your body for x-amount of years. For me, the day I walked into the gym, I had been in my body for thirty-six years. When I walked in the gym and sat for my consult, I told my coach four things: **1.** I played soccer. **2.** I have an injury to my right side **3.** I don't know how to cook. **4.** I don't eat eggs. At that time in my life, that is what I knew about my body, so that's what I communicated.

It is your responsibility to communicate everything you know about your body. A great coach will be listening to everything, even the things you don't say. When I say *communicate everything*, that includes, food preferences, foods that you enjoy but don't agree with you, which forms of exercise have worked well in the past, number of pregnancies, miscarriages, frequency of bowel movements, sleep patterns, etc. Everything. In my experience, it benefitted my coach to know *most* everything.

For me, my coach and I learned together, that my cardio was best done right before bed, like right before bed. The next morning, it actually looked like my body had been working through the night, chiseling and shredding.

This was also where I learned the value of rest and recovery. Recovery *is* a part of the workout. You need to know that. If you switch the order of your meals, if you changed the time of your cardio, tell your coach. Be an *active participant* in your training and in your prep. You know your body; communicate what you know. At the same time, allow your coach do his or her work. Blend the two together and there really isn't a reason you won't come home with a medal. This is a team effort, so participate!

Do you have a contract?

Remember, at the end of the day, the client/coach dynamic has to work for *both* individuals for *you* to achieve results. As a coach, if you are a handful, I don't want to be stuck with you counting down the months until this is over and as a client, you don't want to be stuck with me if I don't deliver. Signing on the dotted line *means nothing* as it relates to your results. If the client/coach dynamic works, it works! A contract is not going to make the relationship more successful.

Pricing?

If you choose to work with your coach for in-person personal training, expect to pay the personal training fees, and then once you shift into a 16-week prep, a different set of fees. You will find a range from about $850-$1900 for a 16-week prep.

These are a set of more prep-specific questions:

As an athlete, do you know your body type?

If you don't know, your coach will better be able to identify it for you. The purpose of your Coach identifying your body type, and the strengths your physique already has, is about being competitive and knowing where your physique will be best represented. New divisions are opening up based on body types. If you are into bodybuilding, then you know about one of the newer categories called Wellness.

Of course, bodybuilding is about balance, but no matter how hard some athletes work to develop their upper bodies, their lower half is just plain ol' nice, just stacked! Their lower body consistently outpaces the upper. This is a specific body type and because of the popularity of athletes with these body types entering the sport, the Wellness division was created.

You should always be striving for balance, but in the meantime, there are divisions where you can start, which allows you to find your feet in the industry. Start in Bikini, even if Women's Figure is your goal. You can still compete in the division appropriate for your *current* physique while you are working on your future self.

When does prep begin?

On more than a few occasions, I've experienced a potential client walking into an initial consultation, sitting down and saying, "I need to lose weight, I want to look like those girls, I want to be in Prep. I need to be in Prep." **Prep does not begin because you say so.**

There is a six months to one year window of relentless consistency that must be executed with your weight lifting program, prepped meals, and sleep! No, you should not be doing fasted cardio right now. Most often, potential clients have the need, "to shed a few pounds and the process of prep", mixed up. These two things are not the same.

Prep begins the day you and your coach identify the date of your show, your coach looks at the calendar, and counts backwards 16-weeks . Your coach marks that date on the calendar and looks up at you and says, "You go into prep on December 12th at 6:00 am." Not one day before, not one day after.

When do you expect your clients to check-in?

Try your best to find a recurring spot on the calendar; my coach and I consistently meet every Wednesday. As prep approaches, expect a bi-weekly meeting. During prep once a week; and closer to your show, every few days.

Do you actually go to the show with your clients?

I know coaches who do both. I know coaches who attend shows with each client. I know coaches who will encourage several of their athletes to compete at one show together; and I know coaches who do not go to shows with their athletes. Of course, having your coach present on show day is ideal. I remember being backstage at a show, and something about this particular competitor did not feel right. I noticed her watching the other athletes a bit more intently than normal. What I was picking up on, was her asking herself, *"Should I be doing that too?"*

I asked her, "Is your coach here?" Her response was, "No." It was her first show, and her coach did not travel with her. Now I was not present for any part of her 16-week prep, therefore, I am not at liberty to speak on anything that happened during that time frame, but I felt sad for her. She was literally wandering around backstage alone, like she didn't know what to do, because she didn't.

Have you competed before?

I do think it is important to have a prep coach who has competed several times before. If you were to hire a professor, you would expect to see textbooks and degrees; a professional bodybuilding/prep coach should have his or her degrees displayed in the form of awards and medals. I can hear some people already saying, "Well what about Iris Kyle, Kai Greene, Ronnie Coleman, or Jay Cutler? They don't compete anymore." Let me clarify: they have seen the mountain top in this sport. Iris

Kyle could coach me through a prep, sipping a Mai Tai in the Canary Islands or from her condo on the moon, and I would do exactly as she says. I'm not talking about that. I'm talking about walking into your local gym, and telling the personal trainers at your local faux-named big box gym, "I want to compete, can you help me?"

Do you have a coach?

Yes, ask. Coaching, in whatever industry keeps everyone accountable. Find a coach who has a coach or at minimum a mentor or professional peer who they bounce ideas off of.

Do you still compete?

If your coach is still competing and has mentioned competing in the same show as you, ask questions. Review the questions on communication, boundaries, and expectations

I've seen this go both ways. I know a few coaches that have gone through a prep with their clients. On one hand, for a first-time competitor, it's a nice gesture to keep them motivated! On the other, prep is an intense personal commitment and demands your selfishness. Is the coach invested in you and able to keep up with your prep, or are they so focused on their own prep that they have lost track of your progress? If your coach is still competing and has mentioned competing in the same show as you, ask questions. Review the questions on communication, boundaries and expectations. It's actually kind of awesome to have your coach compete with you.

How many athletes have you turned Pro?

At first, this question may seem like a judgment on the coach. It isn't meant to be. I learned to ask this question. In my experience, asking gives me an idea of *how long* the coach has been in the game. Every now and again, you will meet an Athlete who wins their Pro Card on the first attempt. In general though, earning a Pro Card is no easy task. If the coach you are thinking about selecting has turned athletes pro, *that coach knows how to prep!* Remember, the fitness industry is a billion dollar industry. For a bodybuilding competition, the Coach you want isn't the one at the gym writing a workout five minutes before a client walks in the door or posting a new booty workout on Instagram. The coach you want **is a master** in his or her lane, and that lane is competition prep!

Are you a Pro in any organization?

This is another question may seem like a judgment, but it isn't. What many people may not know, and this depends on the organization, is that after an athlete earns his or her Pro card, in order for the athlete to maintain Pro status, an athlete must compete every two years. I think it is pretty cool that at some point, your coach may be in the trenches with you!

Do you teach your athletes posing?

Find yourself a reputable coach that teaches his/her athletes posing. If your coach does not teach posing, that is fine, but he or she should have someone on speed dial that does.

As a coach, what is your goal for your athletes?

You need a Coach that isn't just going to take your money and put you in any random show. I've seen it before: an athlete decides she wants to do a large National Physique Committee (NPC) show. She has competed at one local show in a high school auditorium, and now wants to get on stage and compete at the NPC level. At your average local show, you have somewhere between 75-150 athletes. At an NPC show, you will have at minimum 250 athletes registered. If she competes at a local show and does not even place, by numbers alone, what is the likelihood that she will have a positive experience at a larger show?

I know for a fact that some coaches will not advise a first-time natural competitor that the show they have picked to compete in is a non-tested show, where seasoned vets are competing. The coach will let you do what you want to do, and take your money while you are doing it. Sure, you are a free agent and can enter whatever show you please, but there is also something to be said about the integrity of your coach and actually *coaching* you and ensuring that your first experience is a positive one.

And that is when you stop and ask, "As a coach, what is your goal for your athletes?" Just knowing my coach even thought "top three" was clear and realistic, helped me redefine my own expectation of myself; I didn't want to let my coach down, and that goes back to respect.

Asking the aforementioned questions allows you to properly vet your coach. After you have asked all of your questions, your intuition has been satisfied and you decide *this is the coach I want,* it is time to move forward, knowing that you are in good hands. People are shocked when I say I don't ask my coach questions. They respond in disbelief, "You don't ask your coach questions?"

The questioning is over; that part is done. Now it is time for the doing. Most humans I know either overthink, create made up scenarios, or try to think themselves *out* of a situation. You are not supposed to think, you are not supposed to know, you are not supposed to rationalize, you are supposed to do. Remember the elements of a dynamic partnership? Honesty, trust, compassion, integrity, loyalty, and respect. Now, trust emerges.

Let's get to work!

GLOSSARY

Terms you want to become familiar with.

Anterior– Refers to the muscles on the front side of body.

Athletes– Competitors registered for a show can also be referred to as athletes.

Athletes Meeting– An information session that occurs the night before the show or early morning of the show.

Awards Ceremony– Takes place at the night show. Athletes are awarded their medals, also known as hardware.

Amateur Athlete– An athlete in any organization that has not yet been awarded their Pro card.

Amateur Card– Once you've paid your show registration fees and prior to stepping on stage, you will need to purchase a card for the specific organization you are competing in. Unless you've been awarded Pro status, you will purchase your amateur card.

Backstage– Every show is different. But in many cases, if you so desire, you can purchase a backstage pass. Backstage is where all the show day magic happens!

Backstage Shots– This seems to be a new phenomenon. Some shows will use two photographers; one for stage shots and the other for backstage shots. Both photographers are professional quality, but the backstage photographer definitely captures the excitement and fun of the day differently. Backstage shots are pretty cool.

Call Outs– Judges may call athletes out to center stage to perform comparison rounds several times with the same set or a different set of athletes. Hence you will hear an athlete say, "I got first call outs." That's typically a good thing!

Category– If the show promoter decides, each division will have one, two, or maybe three categories for which you may register. You must pay the fees for each category. For example: If your division is Women's Physique, you have the opportunity to register for Novice, Open, and Master. That's three opportunities to win some hardware.

Class– Depending on how many athletes are registered, athletes will be divided into classes, typically by height.

Cobra– Nickname for Men's Rear Lat Flare pose. Flared lats mirror the head of a king cobra about to strike.

Comparison Rounds– Athletes are standing side by side performing the mandatory poses for that specific division. Judges will ask athletes to run through comparison rounds several times.

Competitors– Athletes registered for a show can also be referred to as competitors.

Competition Tan– Typically done by a professional tanning agency. A competition tan is a must for every individual to present their best look. A competition tan highlights, contours and defines muscle.

Dial I – Once your coach learns which training types and foods your body respond positively to, you can begin to do what the industry calls dial in, or making small adjustments. For example: your body prefers 2 ounces of avocado instead of 14 almonds.

That's dialing in. Nuance matters!

Divisions– Women's Physique, Women's Bikini, Women's Figure, Men's Physique, Men's Classic Bodybuilding. When someone asks, "Which division do you compete in?" you'll say, "I compete in Women's Figure."

Division Fees– If you compete in Women's Figure, there are three categories you can enter: Open, Novice, and Master. Each category you register for will cost you approximately $100.

Expeditor– An individual, most often dressed in black, who directs athletes onstage and backstage.

Fans– This term refers to all of your people, your kingdom {or queendom.) And you shall look at them and wave as you receive your hardware.

Fluffy– A bodybuilder's endearing term for fat.

Genetics– The stuff God and your momma gave you. Your moneymaker. These are the features that make your body prime for bodybuilding. Wide back, round shoulders, tiny waist, great calves, and a good booty.

Gold Standard– This is a term that refers to the athlete who the judges look to and compare other bodies to in a specific Division. i.e. Latorya Watts is still the gold standard for Women's Figure.

Ground Up– A term used in posing: begin every single pose by flexing and stabilizing the lower half of your body first.

Hardware– The good stuff. Your medals.

Head Judge– Also called the center judge. The head judge is the voice you will hear most often. He or she will be calling the quarter turns for the athletes.

Judges– On show day, the only people that matter.

Lagging Body Parts– Body parts that just don't seem to get with the program. And when they do get with the program, they don't stay with it. To use myself as an example: my glutes and right tricep are my lagging body parts.

Live Judging– Typically occurs during the evening show when an athlete's placement is in question. The judges will run the athletes through their comparison rounds, and then say something like, "Ladies and gentlemen we are about to go into live judging." After that announcement, the room is silent.

Mirror Muscles– Development of muscles on the front side or top half of the body only.

Muscle Size or **Muscle Development–** This refers to full muscle bellies. At the moment you are being judged, is the muscle as full and developed as it possibly can be?

Morning Show– Synonymous with prejudging.

Order of Events– You will find this list taped on a wall backstage. The Order of Events outlines the order in which the divisions will appear on stage.

Organization– The umbrella under which you chose to compete. For example: GBO (Global Bodybuilding Organization), NPC (National Physique Committee), NFF (Naturally Fit Federation).

Package– Every aspect of your physique and every detail you intend to present to the judges for scoring. Skin tone, the color selection on your finger nails, the precise fit of your posing trunks or suit. The judges are scoring your total package.

Peak Week– Seven days out from show day. This is it! You made it. Stay focused and confidently execute all the knowledge you have acquired.

Pivots– Pivots and quarter turns are synonyms. They are always performed to the right. Always.

Posterior– Refers to the muscles on the backside of body.

Posing Trunks– Specifically refers to Men's divisions. Each Men's Division is required to wear a different style trunk. Be prepared and plan accordingly.

Prejudging– Prejudging occurs during the morning show. Prejudging is the first time judges have a look at all of the competitors together.

Prep– The sixteen-week period in which you and your coach focus primarily on achieving stage ready levels of leanness.

Pro Athlete– An athlete in any organization that has earned Pro Status.

Pro Card– Once you become a Pro, your status changes from Amateur to Pro, therefore you will now possess a Pro Card.

Promoter– The promoter is the owner or the group of individuals who sponsor a show.

Pumping Up– Just before you hit the stage, you will spend several minutes using resistance bands, dumbbells or whatever you have at your disposal to pump up. You are literally pumping up your muscles to show the judges the very best version of symmetry, conditioning and muscle development they have ever seen.

Registration– The money you pay to enter and compete in the show. Ideally, you'll want to pay this fee the moment you enter prep.

Show Day– The day you've been waiting for. Show day is all day: 3am – midnight. Be ready!

Show Promoter– The individuals or group of individuals who promote or own the show.

Slippers or **Slides–** The comfy shoes you get to wear when you're not on stage.

Stage Shots– Professional photos of you and only you center stage.

Symmetry– refers to an even and well-proportioned physique: top to bottom, right to left, back to front.

Stage Time– Stage time is the amount of time a competitor spends on stage. To increase your stage time, a good coach will encourage you to register for all divisions and categories your physique will be competitive in.

Stoning– The official name for the bling on your suit.

Reversing out– The process of taking your body from show day levels of leanness and transitioning your body back to a place of healthy maintenance. In a perfect world, the same way you went in to prep is the same way you will come out.

Robe– When you are not on stage, wrap yourself up in your robe. Stay warm!

The Pivot– Refers to the motion of your feet while setting your body into a quarter turn.

The Pump– The feeling of full and swollen muscles. I really can't think of a better feeling.

Vendors– One of the more fun aspects of a bodybuilding show is the Expo. Vendors are selling just about anything you can think of and there are samples of everything! I remember going to a show in Dallas. I walked into the venue and there was a huge sign that read SARMS* and a free T-shirt. My chin dropped. So, when I say everything, I mean it!

Venue– The location where the show will be held. Example: Metropolitan Event Center

---

*   Selective Androgen Receptor Modulators

PHRASES

Hit your quarter turns– When said with the proper inflection, *hit your quarter turns means* "Show the judges what you've got, do it just like we practiced!"

Hit your pose– The moment you've completed your pivot, your body goes into whatever the first mandatory pose is for your division. This phrase means get into the pose immediately, without delay, and hold it!

Make the judges work– Every show isn't the same. There will be shows you attend where there isn't one single person that stands out as the clear winner. So, you'll hear this phrase from the audience when there is a stacked class. If you are on stage as a competitor and you hear this phrase yelled from the audience, know that the competition is stiff. You better turn your charm all the way on because all of the athletes are meticulously hitting their quarter turns, all of the athletes have come in with quality muscle development, precise symmetry, and conditioning. Every single athlete is standing in the best version of themselves. Now the responsibility is on the judges to work the athletes by running them through comparison rounds and moving the athletes around, round after round. When all of the athletes are exceptional, the judges have to work.

Practice your pivots– This is something your posing coach will say directly to you, or your peers will say to one another. This phrase refers to perfecting your quarter turns.

Pulled to the center/moved to the center– Bodybuilding lore says: once the judges have run the athletes through their mandatory poses and are just about to dismiss them, the athlete standing in the center will be the athlete who wins the category. Go to a show, you decide.

A Stacked Class– the head judge will likely say this phrase. It means there are tons of athletes standing in front of him or her and everyone looks good!

Thinning the Skin– During prep, as your fasted cardio sessions increase, your goal is to lose as much body fat as possible, so that when show day comes and you start to fill up on carbs again, your skin will appear thin. Meaning there is as little fat as possible between the muscle and your skin. Therefore, showing all of your well-developed muscle.

Training on a Split– Training specific body parts on specific days of the week. If you ask a bodybuilder, "What day is today?" and you're expecting "Thursday" as a response, but instead you get "Back day," chances are he or she trains on a split.